THREE PRESS SECRETARIES ON THE PRESIDENCY AND THE PRESS

Jody Powell
George Reedy
Jerry terHorst

Edited by
Kenneth W. Thompson

UNIVERSITY
PRESS OF
AMERICA

LANHAM • NEW YORK • LONDON

THREE PRESS SECRETARIES
ON THE PRESIDENCY AND THE PRESS:
Jody Powell
George Reedy
Jerry terHorst

VOLUME V IN A SERIES
FUNDED BY THE
JOHN and MARY R. MARKLE FOUNDATION

Copyright © 1983 by

University Press of America,™ Inc.

4720 Boston Way
Lanham, MD 20706

3 Henrietta Street
London WC2E 8LU England

Printed in the United States of America

Library of Congress Cataloging in Publication Data

Main entry under title:

Three press secretaries on the presidency and the press.

 1. Presidents—United States—Press conferences.
2. Government and the press—United States. I. Powell,
Jody. II. Reedy, George E., 1917-   . III. TerHorst,
Jerald F. IV. Thompson, Kenneth W., 1921-   .
V. Title: 3 press secretaries on the presidency and the
press.

JK518.T47   1983   353.03'5   83-16804
ISBN 0-8191-3576-3 (alk. paper)
ISBN 0-8191-3577-1 (pbk. : alk. paper)

THREE PRESS SECRETARIES
ON THE PRESIDENCY AND THE PRESS:
Jody Powell
George Reedy
Jerry terHorst

Dedicated
to the
Council
of
The Miller Center
and its
chairman
Governor Linwood Holton

TABLE OF CONTENTS

PREFACE

A wise friend once remarked: "In study and research as in baseball, you score runs by bunching hits." The Miller Center in its studies and colloquia has undertaken to follow this axiom. With assistance from the John and Mary R. Markle Foundation it has sought to illuminate certain major issues concerning the presidency and the media that have been of widespread public concern in the recent past. These studies have resulted in the following publications:

1. *Report of the Commission on Presidential Press Conferences* co-chaired by Governor Linwood Holton and Ray Scherer;
2. *The Presidential Press Conference: Its History and Role in the American Political System* by Blaire Atherton French;
3. *Ten Presidents and the Press* edited by Kenneth W. Thompson; and
4. *The White House Press on the Presidency: News Management and Cooption* edited by Kenneth W. Thompson.

The present volume should be seen as a companion volume to the previous volume involving senior members of the White House press. The two volumes are intended to help Americans understand the President's relation with the press and view it in clearer perspective. A final comparative volume is in preparation treating the relationship of presidents, prime ministers, heads of state and the press in the United States and other countries.

1

INTRODUCTION

As we set about organizing the fifth volume in the Miller Center series on the presidency and the press, we invited opinions from members of our national commission and from others with whom we consulted on the quality of press secretaries in the post war era. The name which was first on almost everyone's list was that of the late James Hagerty, President Eisenhower's press secretary. We might have wished that the timing of an inquiry such as ours would have made possible Mr. Hagerty's participation. We note that all too often history has a way of bypassing good intentions. In other programs, we have tried to reach senior people whose days may be numbered.

Fortunately, two other well-respected press secretaries with rather long tenures were also high in the rankings of those who responded to our question. Jody Powell of Vienna, Georgia, served as press secretary throughout President Jimmy Carter's administration. Although he did not have an earlier journalistic background, he gained the plaudits of the White House press corps and became a familiar figure on television and throughout the country presenting President Carter's views. Beyond having personal qualities of a high order, Powell had the trust and confidence of the President throughout his four years in office. George Reedy's standing was based on somewhat different credentials. A long time aide and associate of Lyndon B. Johnson, his relationship to the President as press secretary ultimately led to a break and to his departure. Yet few would contest the fact that Mr. Reedy remains one of the most articulate interpreters of the presidency and the press serving currently as Nieman Professor of Journalism at Marquette University. He has also written two important books, *The Twilight of the Presidency* (1970) and *The Presidency in Flux* (1973). Jerry terHorst, now with the Ford Motor Company, had only a short-lived tenure as press secretary to President Gerald Ford. They parted company because of differences of opinion over the pardon by Ford of President Richard M. Nixon. However no one has a higher reputation for integrity among journalists and press secretaries than Mr. terHorst. The three press secretaries spent a day and a half at the Miller Center in lectures, forums and discussion.

The first selection in the volume grew out of a lecture in the Dome Room of the Rotunda by Jody Powell. Mr. terHorst and Mr. Reedy commented both on Mr. Powell's general subject and his paper. The extent of community and university interest in press relations was reflected in the lively responses of an overflow crowd in the beautiful Dome Room. In his paper, Mr. Powell called for greater realism and responsibility on the part of reporters as well as politicians. Realism should be based on a clear-eyed recognition of the role of profits for the media and politics for the politician. He also maintained that neither decision makers nor reporters know what an action means in terms of its full context and consequences. Yet every night on the 6:00 news, they speak as if they knew. Responsibility for journalists should involve admitting their frailties and mistakes, much as they judge political leaders on this basis.

The second major part of the volume resulted from a day long colloquium between the three press secretaries, Virginia journalists and political scientists from the University of Virginia. The former included James Latimer, dean of political columnists for the *Richmond Times-Dispatch,* Staige Blackford, editor of the *Virginia Quarterly Review* and formerly press secretary for Governor Linwood Holton, Felicia Warburg Rogan, and Jean Scott of Charlottesville. Among the political scientists were James Sterling Young, Charles O. Jones, David Clinton, Larry Sabato and Blaire French, all of the University.

The participants rang the changes on a host of issues and questions prepared by Mr. Clinton and myself. These included:

What are the requirements for the success of a press secretary?

What was your conception of the office when you came in and when you left?

What changes do you wish you had made?

What formats can the President use other than presidential press conferences?

How did you and he select one or the other?

What was the attitude of the press corps toward you and the President? Did it change?

What was the President's attitude toward the press? What were the sources? Did he change?

Was there a conflict in your role in serving two masters, the President and the press?

Did you see evidence of news management and cooption? Does the press exaggerate? Is their concern valid? Who is coopting whom?

How did you seek to improve relations with the press? Did you succeed? Did the President?

Must the relation between President and press be adversarial?

How do you react to the press' claim that their only goal is to seek the truth?

What advice would you give to future press secretaries?

The volume concludes with two essays by George E. Reedy. We are grateful to the editors of the *Annals* of the American Academy of Political and Social Science and to the *Public Communication Review* at the School of Public Communication at Boston University for permission to reprint these articles.

THE RELATIONSHIP OF THE PRESIDENT AND THE PRESS

Jody Powell

MR. THOMPSON: At the end of each administration, press secretaries may not be the man of the year. Yet this audience by your presence testifies to the fact that they are a very visible part of the American government and an important one as time has gone on. We are privileged to have three press secretaries representing both political parties who will speak and discuss issues connecting the relationship of the President and the press.

It is my pleasure first to introduce Mr. George Reedy, who was press secretary to President Lyndon Baines Johnson. Mr. Reedy.

MR. REEDY: I'm beginning at this moment to recognize some of the real delights of having been a press secretary. I can assure you when I was press secretary I never got a warm outburst of applause whenever I mounted the rostrum. The world's greatest hero to the press is a preceding press secretary and the world's greatest villain—a combination of Mephistopheles, Beelzebub, and Satan—is the one now in office.

I'm going to make my introduction of these two gentlemen rather brief. I learned a long time ago that one does not have to be eternal in order to be immortal. But I do want to say a few general words about the concept of a press secretary of the White House. It is a very new position in historic terms. The full-fledged press secretary, such as the three that you see before you right now, are creatures not only of the twentieth century but creatures of about the last fifty years. The job really originated with Roosevelt. Herbert Hoover did have a man designated to collect written questions from the press. But he did not answer anything. At certain periods Mr. Hoover would appear before

7

the press and read written answers—that is, written answers to those that he wished to answer—and that was that.

The press secretary is a modern institution and it began, in my judgment, because under Franklin Delano Roosevelt, the President of the United States for the first time in history became very close to us. It was a strange world before Roosevelt. A President was somebody that you thought about in times of war and in times of an election campaign because he was entertaining. Those were the days when your entertainment was limited to presidential campaigns or the Chautaqua circuit or an occasional circuit-riding preacher.

But relations between the President and the press go way back, back to the beginning, back to George Washington. And they started out on an adversarial basis. We are meeting in an institution that owes very much to a certain gentleman who in the early days of the Republic owned a newspaper in Washington, D.C. I'm talking about Mr. Thomas Jefferson. He never admitted he owned the newspaper but there was very little doubt about the sponsorship. There was also another gentleman in the Cabinet named Alexander Hamilton who also had a newspaper appeared with a series of articles signed Publius, Veritas, Tribunux, Pro Bono Publico, pseudonyms like that. In the Hamiltonian paper Mr. Jefferson was a man whose personal habits were so filthy that Washington housewives would not invite him into their homes for fear that the grease on his hair would ruin the anti-macassars on their chairs. And in the Jefferson paper Mr. Hamilton was a man who had an undue relationship with a number of slave girls. As you can see, in those days journalism was really rough. The situation got so bad that George Washington finally called the two in and said in effect, "For the love of God, cool it, you're making the whole administration look bad."

Since then there has been a long history of an adversarial relationship between the President and the press. There are only two men who have ever escaped it. One was Jerry Ford, who is an awfully nice guy and who had not been elected to the office. (I think the election is an ordination as well as a selection process.) The other is William Henry Harrison who died after one month in the office. Aside from that every President has gotten into a fight with the press and what happened, I think, at the time of Roosevelt is that there was a desire to put a buffer between the President and the press so some of the fiercer blows could be absorbed by the press secretary, that is, the blows coming from the press. On the other hand the President realized that it might be as well to have somebody to soften some of his fiercer blows directed at the press.

Since then there has been a long list of people, some of them quite distinguished, some of them middling—like most things the real world is divided between a few, a very few saints, a very few real sinners, and a lot of people who are tolerable. And I think that we who are in the class of press secretaries reflect just about the same—maybe a couple of saints, maybe a couple of sinners, a lot of people who are tolerable.

But the important point that I want to impress upon you before I leave the stage, is that as you listen to press secretaries, I believe you are going to discover that fundamentally the differences between them are the differences among the Presidents. A press secretary to a President is not the same thing as a minister of information in a parliamentary government. There is a bad confusion over that point—a confusion shared by much of the press. It amounts to a belief that the job of the press secretary is to decide what information shall go to the public and what information shall not. Believe me that is not his job. He is there for one purpose and one purpose only, that is to speak for the President. And he can't speak any other way because of the nature of our government. We only have one President. Don't forget this: the press secretary only had one vote for his job, the man for whom he is speaking had tens of millions of votes, so consequently there is no doubt whatsoever as to whom he speaks for.

How he handles the job is only going to be partially a reflection of his own individual ability or his own relationships with the press. I think that we have had some very fine press secretaries who in my judgment never got the recognition they were entitled to simply because their relationship with the President broke down. We have had other cases where the relationship held up, and the one thing that is essential in my judgment, the one quality a press secretary must have is a very close, fine relationship with the President. I think you've got all the gamut here—you got me who started out with a very good relationship with a President that fell to pieces after a short period of time. The next gentleman you are going to hear had a very fine relationship with the President and consequently did a very fine job. The gentleman that you hear at the other end, I think was equally capable but he got head-on with the President very early. They started butting heads at an early period.

You must remember at all times, then, that the press secretary is there to speak for the President. He is not there to make decisions on what the press shall print or shall not print. I have actually run into Americans when I was press secretary that thought I could forbid the newspapers to print something. Hah! Or thought I could forbid the television cameras to carry something—none of that.

9

Now first as soon as I finish being prolix and wordy—we are going to present Jody Powell who was press secretary under President Carter. And I think that one of Jody's great assets is that he did sustain a good relationship with the President of the United States during all the time that he was in office—and not only sustained that relationship but also did a good job because I think he understood the position. Today Jody is writing a column a couple of times a week for the *Dallas Times Herald*, the *Los Angeles Times* Syndicate and he's working on a book on White House press relations. (If it's any good, Jody, I'll make my class buy it.) In addition to that he is acting as a consultant in various capacities for TV and various types of public affairs programs.

After that we are going to have some comments. We never allow a press secretary to appear before the public without being challenged somewhere along the line. And the challenger today is going to be Jerry terHorst, a very old friend of mine back in the days before we became press secretaries. Jerry was press secretary for a very brief period to President Jerry Ford, and I think that Mr. Ford lost because he did not extend the period. But the difficulty is that Jerry and Mr. Ford had a rather important disagreement and I think if I had to pass judgment on it I'd say that Jerry was right but to be right against a President is the same thing as to have a nickel. When you make a telephone call any more, it costs twenty-five cents. To be honest the President plus a nickel will will get you a telephone call thirty years ago. You learn very early that in the White House there can be very heated arguments but you know who's going to win. And so with that, having taken up too much time already, I'm going to present to you Mr. Jody Powell.

MR. POWELL: I appreciate the opportunity to be here and let me say too that I remember coming to Washington six years or so ago knowing even less about the White House and the government and press secretaries' responsibilities than I do now. People like George Reedy and Jerry terHorst and many others who had held that position prior to the time that I got there were absolutely unstinting in their willingness to sit down and talk, to give me the benefit of their best and, I think, frank advice, and I might say that most of my mistakes were not a result of those conversations. As a matter of fact if I had had enough sense to know what they were talking about, my time in the White House would have been much more successful and certainly I probably would have missed a few stump holes that I stepped in along the way.

I want to talk about the press White House relationships for a few minutes today, but probably a little but more about the press than the White House. It is something I like to do although it's a bit of a awkward position for me to be in, talking about the press. It's a little bit like the fellow who had been sentenced to hang who was asked by the judge who had just done the sentencing if he had anything he wanted to say. The fellow said, "Well, your Honor, I know there are many people in this community who think well of you." He said, "Your Honor, I know there are some people in this community that admire and even respect you. But your Honor, I got to tell you the truth, you have went and ruined yourself with me." Hopefully what I have to say in the next few minutes will show you that my view is not quite that jaundiced with regard to the press, but maybe not.

One of the things that the past couple of years being outside the White House has done for me is to give me a much finer appreciation for our American political system and the political process in this country. In many nations on the face of this earth, when the people rise up and throw you out of office, they then stand you up against a wall and shoot you. Here in the United States they send you out on the lecture circuit, and I'll be glad to let you know which system I consider to be the more humane after we get through with the question and answer period.

Speaking of questions and answers, the one question that I used to get more often than any other is: what is it that a press secretary actually does? As a matter of fact the person who asked that question most frequently was the President. I never was able to come up with an answer that completely satisfied him or me but there is an illustration that might help to explain it a little bit better. When I was growing up in a little town in south Georgia, one of the highlights of the year, and there weren't a whole lot of highlights, was when the traveling circus came to town, which gives you some feel for how long ago it was. Circuses still travelled, and not only that but they travelled to towns as small as Vienna, Georgia. It was a wonderful time; they would come usually in the fall after crops had been gathered. They would come in usually on Thursday night or Friday morning. They'd spend all day Friday getting things set up and then Friday afternoon before the first big show they'd have a parade, a wonderful thing. People would come in from the whole county, line the sidewalks, stand there. It seemed to me to be one of most amazing spectacles I'd ever witness. You'd have clowns, you'd have a band, you'd have semi-wild animals in cages rolling by, you'd have elephants marching trunk to tail, you'd have semi-beautiful ladies on white horses riding by— wonderful thing. After all that had gone by, if you stood there long enough, after a while you would see a sort of scruffy looking guy coming along usually with a half-pint in his back pocket with a bucket and a shovel—that guy was a press secretary.

I have gone through an interesting, at least for me, metamorphosis in the past couple of years too from about ten years plus as a press secretary and a government spokesman to now being ivolved in the commentating and columnizing business. As a friend of mine said it was like someboy who had spent his whole life as a doctor suddenly decided he wanted to become a disease. Another one reminded me that I had once described newspaper columnists as the sort of people who view the conflict from afar and then come down out of the hills to shoot the wounded. Be that as it may, one of the benefits I think of these past two years, is that it has given me a different and I hope more accurate and objective perspective on the relationship that we are here to talk about today. A great deal has been written and said for years about the relationship of Presidents and just about every institution in our society—the Congress, the bureaucracy, political parties, interest groups, international organizations, first ladies, you name it. But at least until the last few years surprisingly little study has been devoted to the relationship that I think could be as important as any that a President conducts with any institution in our society, and that is a President's relationship with the press.

✓ Part of the reason I think that relationship is so important has to do with what I think to be the role of the President. It seems to me that if you had to pick one primary responsibility for a President it would be the molding and shaping of our national attitudes and opinions into some sort of coherent public policy. That's a President's job because the President is the one single individual who has a shot at doing that. Only a President can remind us every now and then of the importance of thinking through the long-range consequences of those ideas that might seem so appealing at the moment. And when passions rage or indifference triumphs, it's only a President who can hold us back or push us on just a little bit. Only a President in our political system can effectively appeal to the best that's within us when we are tempted to yield to the worst, and only he can lift our vision and remind us of our obligations to the common good and the general welfare, the sort of obligations that, at least occasionally, ought to transcend our fascination with personal, private, and particular interests. To paraphrase someone who had a great deal of experience in molding and lifting the vision of people, "How shall they believe in what they have not heard and how shall they hear without a preacher?" And I guarantee you if Saint Paul had worked in the White House he surely would have asked, "And how shall the preacher be heard except through the press?"

I've always thought that the ability of a President to shape and move a nation is in fact greatly exaggerated both in the minds of many in the press and in the President's mind, at least on that first day when he walks into the Oval Office. I happen to think, perhaps somewhat cynically, that this exaggerated perception of presidential power may be encouraged by some in the fourth estate. It does after all contribute to the idea of the press as a courageous little David, taking on the Goliath in the Oval Office, and it is sometimes used to justify excess and shoddy performance on the part of journalists.

✓ As you may have guessed, I think the relationship between press and President is basically flawed. I don't think it works the way that it should. I think it doesn't work well in that it fails to provide the public with that quality and quantity of information that they have a right to expect and that they need in order to make the decisions that are necessary to self-government. And that, it seems to me, is the role of the press. If you can define the role of a press secretary, it falls somewhere in that connection between the responsibility of the press to transmit the quality of information that's needed for self-government and a responsibility of the President to lead us.

I think that the reason the relationship between press and President is flawed relates to both institutions, the press and the White House, and the problems relate much more to institutional pressures and constraints that play upon both the people who work in the White House and people who are trying to cover the people who work in the White House. Then, too, the individuals themselves. The problems are not primarily the product of malice or bias on the part of reporters, although there is some of that, nor are they chiefly caused by dishonesty and deceit by people in the White House, although that also crops up now and then. In fact the more I have had a chance to think about it the more I have been struck by the basic similarity between the sort of pressures and constraints that White House reporters and White House staffers have to deal with.

A few examples: Both institutions, the press and the White House, operate against artificial deadlines which may have only a coincidental relationship at best to what's happening in the real world. On top of that both institutions have to be sensitive, not only to their own deadlines, but to the deadlines of the other. No press operation in the White House can function obviously without a keen understanding of how much time it takes the networks to get a story on the air, of when the final copy deadline for the edition of the *New York Times* that is distributed in Washington might be, and so forth. No White House correspondent can operate successfully in the White House without an understanding of the general pace and schedule of decision-making, the flow of paper, the way that the actors behave, including the President.

Both institutions almost routinely make decisions based upon inadequate and sometimes woefully inadequate information. In fact I would say that you can almost define a presidential decision as one that is made without enough information to offer a clear choice among the options. And if that is the situation the President faces, you can understand the difficulty that a reporter faces as he or she attempts to explain or even to determine not just what the President has decided, but why he chose this particular option and what the implications of that option may be for the society and indeed for the world a few years or even a few months down the road.

Sometimes I think that journalists would be better off not trying to do just that sort of thing. I remember sitting in that office in the West Wing of the White House, late on many afternoons looking out over the North Lawn and there stood Sam and Judy and Lesley with that beautiful flood-lit North Portico as a backdrop doing their pieces for the evening news. Now I could see them but I couldn't hear what they were saying, although I would hear it soon enough, too soon in many cases. But in most cases I knew pretty close what they were going to be saying toward the end of that minute ten, minute twenty, whatever it was. Somewhere right at the end they were going to try to tell the American people what it all really meant. And that was a frightening thing for me because I knew and they knew, and they knew that I knew that they didn't know what it all really meant. And to make matters worse, on occasion I knew that they were depending on what I had said a few hours earlier to decide what it all really meant. And I also knew that neither I nor the President nor any other mortal on the face of God's earth knew what it all really meant by five-thirty or six o'clock on that particular afternoon. Sam and Judy and Lesley didn't do that because they were perverse, although they could be perverse on occasion, all three of them. They did it because that was what the institution required and, to be frank, because that is what the institution thought, rightly or wrongly, that you/we/us the American people wanted.

Another similarity between the two institutions is that both are influenced by forces which neither is willing to fully acknowledge: money and profit in the case of the fourth estate, politics in the case of the White House. I don't happen to think that there is anything particularly wrong with either. Politics is not a dirty word to me. It is after all how we've decided in this society to link public opinion on the one hand and public policy on the other. The only systems I know of that don't have any politics involved are those in which public opinion and the wishes of the governed don't really make a damn anyway. I think politics is a legitimate consideration in White House decision-making. But I guarantee you I certainly never would have said what I just said two and a half years ago. You don't talk about it, you don't come out to the podium in the White House and say, "Amongst the factors that were considered when the President was trying to make up his mind what he wanted to do about 'X' was how folks are going to react in New Hampshire and besides that we got the folks on the Hill and they're worried about where they are going to get this carrier refurbished." You don't talk about that.

By the same token there is nothing wrong with journalism worrying about money and profit. Except for public broadcasting, newspapers, television, radio, other forms of media are not in the public service business. They can't operate if they don't make money, and they won't make money unless they can sell news in the sense that it is interesting enough that people will watch it or read it, and you can sell ads and you can stay in business. But in like manner, even though that introduces its legitmate concern, it also introduces a bias in the coverage, primarily a bias in the direction of making stories more interesting. You won't find many reporters or journalists standing up talking about the role of that consideration in the journalistic product. The problem is not that the considerations exist but that they exist in that twilight world where they are seldom recognized officially, they are seldom discussed, and it becomes almost impossible to make any real decisions about whether, in a particular instance, they are exercising a proper or an improper sort of role.

A result of that lack of consideration is a degree of cynicism that is quite unhealthy on the part of the public toward both the press and the government. I think it's a fairly frequent occasion when sensational, and there is nothing wrong with sensation if it's legitimate, sensational but nevertheless important stories are dismissed by readers or viewers as "Well, they're just trying to sell newspapers." And I think in like manner that in many cases government actions that are in fact the product of thoughtful and conscientious consideration are denigrated as "Well, he's just trying to get himself re-elected."

I want to make one final point about similarities, which is to me the most important. Both institutions, I think, have a tendency to become overly hostile and defensive when under attack. As a result both institutions fail to punish mistakes and incompetence to the extent that they should. You've all heard for years about the familiar "circle your wagons" tendency in the White House. You should also know that the "circle your typewriters" exercise in the press corps is about as common when the press is under attack.

I don't want to beat a dead horse here but looking back just a year or so ago to the famous Janet Cooke episode with the *Washington Post,* the one thing that struck me about all that was said and written about that rather embarrassing episode was a story that quoted a number of people who worked there at the *Post,* and one of them said, "You know, we had a lot of questions about this thing for days, weeks. As soon as we saw it there was a lot of talk around the newsroom that this smells funny, it just doesn't look right, it's just a little too neat, it fits together too well. How do you imagine she got it?"—all the sort of questions that a bright, probing journalist who had dealt with trying to get a tough story before would ask. But then the person said, "Then the mayor attacked the story. He said he didn't believe it. And of course all that talk ceased at the paper and we rallied behind our story and our reporter."

God knows that happens in government, too. It happens in the White House too, but it also happens in the fourth estate. And if anything, I think that problem is worse in journalism than it is in government, and I'll tell you why. At least in government there is a system in which the government is embedded and that system, of which the press is a very important part, does work to probe, to discover, to expose and thereby to punish mistakes and incompetence. The press as an institution does not operate in any such system and for that reason it is more likely, in my judgment, that mistakes and incompetence will go unpublished and uncorrected, and that those who are occasionally afflicted by malice or other less laudable emotions will continue to exercise their influence than in the government.

A list of problems makes the next step, I suppose, a solution or two. I am somewhat tempted by the approach that Will Rogers once took in a similar situation. He was advising President Wilson on how to deal with submarines during the First World War, and he said, "Mr. President, all you have to do is bring the Atlantic Ocean to a boil. I'll leave the details to the technicians." Well, I'll do a little bit better than that. One of the topics that comes up most frequently at various seminars and symposia on the press and government is whether the fourth estate can at the same time be both competitive and responsible. Well, I happen to believe it can, although I admit in that regard I'm a little bit like one of my Southern Baptist brethren who was asked if he believed in infant baptism. "Believe it, hell," he said, "I've seen it done." Well, I can't say I've ever seen this done, but I believe in it nevertheless.

Consider the possibility that maybe what we need is not less competition, but more. And when I talk about competition I mean real competition; frankly, the sort of competition that I have enjoyed for a number of years in politics. Competition, first of all, recognizes the tremendous power of the fourth estate. One of the easiest cop-outs when anybody begins to point out our transgressions and our faults is to say, "Well, we're really not that important, don't have much influence, therefore, our errors and shortcomings aren't worth much discussion." The fourth estate, in my view, not only is powerful but it is not hanging on by its fingernails in this country. The First Amendment is not in danger of imminent repeal or evisceration.

In that light, it seems to me that what the press could stand more of is competition that involves a willingness to take the gloves off and tell the truth about your competitor. If he habitually lies, say so; if he doesn't do his homework and is cavalier with the truth, say so. In short, I think both the press and the public would be well served if the fourth estate applied something like the same standards of ethics and competence to their fellow journalists as they do to other major figures and other powerful institutions.

If the *New York Times* makes a major error in an important story, why shouldn't the *Washington Post* be interested in telling us why. If CBS blows its coverage of a major event and tens of millions of people are thereby misinformed, why shouldn't ABC help to answer the public's legitimate questions about how that happened, who was responsible and what is being done, if anything, to try to make sure that it doesn't happen again. If it's news that a congressman is sleeping with his secretary, maybe it ought to be news if an important editor or columnist is doing the same thing. If the public has a right to know, and they certainly do in this case, when someone who is involved in the making of energy policy has a financial conflict of interest, is in a position to profit personally by the shape and the nature of the policy that he or she is helping to form, doesn't the public have a similar right to know? If someone who covers energy policy and thereby helps to determine its final form and shape, almost as surely as many of the policymakers, has a similar conflict, I think the public does have that right. If you enjoy reading pieces about the ten dumbest congressmen in Washington, think how much fun it would be to read a similar piece about the ten dumbest columnists in Washington. Now that, I guarantee you, would be a horse race. It would require a photo finish to separate out the top five.

I still have a little card that was given to me by a very senior and experienced State House corresspondent when I first walked into the governor's office in Georgia. And it says, "It takes a strong democracy to survive a free press." Well, that is undeniably true, but it is also equally true that no democracy can survive without an active and aggressive and free press. That has got to be preserved because if we lose that, everything that we value and cherish and care about in terms of representative government in this country will also eventually be lost. If I turn out to be wrong in something I said earlier—that is, in my view that a free press is secure in this country— I'll be wrong not because of constructive or even unreasonable criticism from former flaks like me, but because the fourth estate has contracted that disease which is most certain to be fatal to any major institution in our society and that is an overriding arrogance that leads to a continuing and massive loss of public confidence and trust. For our sake as a society—forget about the newspapers and the television networks—that must not be allowed to happen. I think it is a responsibility for all of us to understand the ultimate importance of a free press as well as some of its shortcomings and to do what we can to make sure that it doesn't happen. Thank you.

MR. TERHORST: Thank you, Jody. Let me add my compliments to you to those of the audience. I want to start out at the outset to let you know that although I worked for a Republican President and Jody worked for a Democratic one, you see before you two men who have gone through hell, fire, and brimstone together at different periods. Once a marine, always a marine, I learned, and I'll be doggoned if I'm going to stand here and tell you that Jody Powell's problems as press secretary were because he worked for a President of the other party than I worked for. That is simply not the case and if George Reedy were still here I am sure he would reinforce that.

I think there is one especially important thing, though, that we're discussing here today—and I've been making a few notes while Jody was talking, and I'm going to keep them as brief as I can. I think the thing to remember essentially is that the relationship between press secretaries and the press at the White House and the relationships bewteen Presidents and the press at the White House or on the campaign trail or wherever, in some ways is a little bit like what Mark Twain once said about music: "It isn't always as bad as it sounds." There are good things to be said for the relationship that has sprung up during the years.

George Reedy, when he was here, mentioned the really vicious attacks that rival papers owned by Jefferson and Hamilton had made on each other in the early days of the Republic, and I'm sure many of you have heard the phrase "yellow journalism." There was a time in American history, not so long ago as a matter of fact, when important publishers and editors, men of position and wealth and money, literally hired journalistic "hit men," as it were, to bring down politicians and turn governmental decisions in their own favor. One nice fact to remember this afternoon—if we remember nothing else—is that we have come a long way in this country from those days to this so that we can sit here, representing not only the two great parties in the country but, in a university setting, and consider some of the ethical questions involved in press versus presidential relationships. I think that is a very healthy sign about the state of our democracy and I'm sure Jody would agree with me that this is something we think—I certainly think—that is growing rather than lessening.

I, too, share Jody's great concern about press responsibility. One of my favorite off-hand remarks that I happen to think is true, is that a press will not long remain free if it isn't also responsible. If there are attacks on the press generally, they tend to come because the press has erred in this field of responsibility, it has muffed the ball, it has in effect not lived up to its mission. We expect certain things from preachers in our society, priests and members of the clergy, in the same way we expect things from our journalists. We require them, at least I do and I'm sure many of you do, to live up to a certain standard in performance of their work. O.K., you can have a plumber that you have to call back and fix something because it wasn't done right, or you can buy a car and it has to be recalled because of defects. But we don't really want that to happen in newspapers and we feel kind of badly if we find out we've been betrayed on a story. Janet Cooke's story is a classic example of a press betrayal and the fact that it made so much impact, not only on other journalists—perhaps, as Jody says, not enough in some cases—but that it made so much impact on the public tells us that we do expect, we do hold a higher standard than we hold for many other craftsmen.

It is sometimes said about those who are in the press—and I have to tell you that I covered the White House for fifteen years before I became press secretary and have been a journalist most of my life until just a couple of years ago—that one of the cliches, of course, is that reporters are sent out by editors to go to the White House, for example, and listen to Jody Powell and Jerry terHorst and then separate the wheat from the chaff and probably print the chaff. That happens and sometimes we kid each other about that. You cannot get away from that sort of problem.

I think the thing to remember is that a press secretary's role, as George Reedy mentioned at the outset, is to speak for the President of the United States. If he can do that well, he will survive if his President survives. There is no such thing as a popular press secretary and an unpopular President. The reverse is very likely to happen, that is, an unpopular press secretary with a popular President. Usually the two go hand in hand. Quite often the best press secretary in the White House is the President himself. If he's on the same wave length with the public, chances are that relationships between the press secretary and the press, and more importantly between the President and the public, will be on the plus side.

Jody spoke, and I would like to reinforce it, of the limits on the press. We hear a lot—and I used the argument myself, although I hope I didn't use it in a flip way or in a manner when it wasn't called for—we do tend in the press to be very defensive about what we do and resist challenge to our integrity or to our responsibility or to our purpose. Even though we know that perhaps the deadline came upon us before the story was ready—and we let it go anyway. One of the famous lines on the paper that I worked for when the deadline time came was, "All right, every body, let's go with what you've got." And that was it. You went with what you had and you hoped you could fix it up tomorrow. Well, when you cover the President, the public doesn't know that there may be more to that story that you wish you had had time to get but didn't have, or that was unavailable right then. The public is left hanging, as it were, with an incomplete story. That is a measure of responsibility that the press genuinely has not fulfilled to my satisfaction.

There are other limits too. Jody mentioned the profit motive. There isn't a newspaper or a broadcasting station or a network in this country that will remain in business a minute if it didn't make a dollar. And when newspapers fold it's not because they're tired of covering news; it's because they can't make money at the process.

Another thing I think worth remembering is that the size of news staffs, whether you're talking about the *Washington Post* or the *New York Times* or ABC network or the paper in Charlottesville, is never geared to the news that needs to be covered. They have no relationship to each other. The size of a news staff is always geared to how much we can afford to pay. How much money do we have after we bring in the ads, pay the printers, pay the circulation people, put aside a generous amount for debt retirement, perhaps put even a more generous amount aside for the publisher. Then we'll see how much we have left to hire reporters and editors, and how big a hole we'll have to wrap the news around the necessary advertising. Journalists, and I'm one who will plead guilty of this, love to talk about the "calling" of the trade. It certainly is a calling, but as you know preachers don't stay in churches unless there is some money in the collection box, and its the same way wth the calling of your journalists. Nobody works for free in this world, or not for very long.

I'd just like to mention one other thing and that is: there is a great confusion, I think, in the public's mind and sometimes in the minds of members of the press about what is true. There are many times when something is newsy but may not necessarily be truthful. I know that's hard to grasp at first hearing, but if you think about it for a minute you can think of many stories that you can remember that were big events when they occurred which later proved not to be true. Now that isn't the journalist's fault. The journalist's fault—sure he must seek the truth, but essentially he has to go to sources to provide him with the truth. If the source is wrong that doesn't make the journalist at fault— it makes the source wrong. So journalists really have to remember that while they like to talk of this business as a calling, truth and news are not always the same. Hopefully they will be the same most of the time but they are not necessarily always the same. The journalist's calling is to collect facts and to bring them together, and as Walter Lippmann used to say, "Present them in a spotlight so that people can form a reasonable opinion about the facts." And beyond that you really can not expect and should not expect the press to do more for you. Unfortunately it has to be said, I think, that quite often politicians expect the press to do more than that and quite often the press also suspects that it has the ability to do more than give you news. It sometimes thinks that it, by God, is the Bible when it is not.

I would just like to close with one brief comment if I may—two comments. I don't know if any of you saw the Shoe cartoon by Jeff McNelly the other day in which he had a chap who was being handed his coat and his scarf and his gloves and his cane, and another person said, "Here's your car, sir." And some little character asked the wise old owl, "Who was that?" He said, "I don't know, I guess a public servant." In other words, this person was being waited on hand and foot but we call him a public servant. Well, in many ways, you know, the same question legitimately can be asked of members of the press. They are favored in our society. I mean a press card can get you places that ordinary mortals don't always go. A responsibility goes with that, with that ability to get to the White House, to be able to stand two feet from the President's desk. To be that close to a moment in history is not given to everybody, and that to me imposes a responsibility on those we have trusted to be our representatives at that scene. And that's where I think we often encounter a breakdown in the communication between the President and the public through his press secretary and through the press—the intermediaries in our society.

Somebody at our conversations earlier today at the Center asked what comprised an ideal press secretary, and I would like just to close with this. I've thought about it on the way over and I think perhaps the ideal press secretary would be someone who grew up in the South or the Southwest, from a very humble background, who was educated in the East, preferably Harvard or Yale, had mastered the classics, had a degree in economics, had the soul of a poet—and the stamina of a John Riggins.

Thank you very much.

MR. THOMPSON: I think it was Plato who said, "The unexamined life is not worth living." It's been fairly obvious since five p.m. last evening for those of us at the Miller Center that our guests today have tried to follow the implicit guidance that Plato sought to give people. In other words, they have tried to make an unusually stubborn attempt to think clearly about their own task and their own profession, so we are very grateful for that.

We have a few minutes for questions and I wonder who would like to ask the first question.

QUESTION: You said you thought an editor sleeping with his or her secretary should be as much a news story as a congressman doing the same thing. Don't you think that because taxpayers are funding the salaries of both the congressman and his or her staff that it makes a big difference?

MR. POWELL: The question was in regard to that comment which, let me say in my defense, was intended to be somewhat facetious about whether or not it might not be just as much news if an editor was sleeping with his secretary or her secretary as a member of Congress. Well, yes, I think, and if you go back I was careful to say, to talk about something *like* the same standards of ethics and ethical conduct. To deal with that particular question the general distinction is made with, "Well, the congressman's secretary is being paid by taxpayer's funds and that's what's the big deal about it." Well, you know very well that ain't what's the big deal about it. What's interesting to people, why it gets in the newspaper is because people are interested in stuff like that, and I guarantee you if you ran a story of similar nature about Walter Cronkite or David Broder—let me say I know nothing about the private lives of either of them—it would be equally titillating. My only point, if there was a point to that particular comment was that I think journalism to some extent would be well served by walking a mile on occasion in the shoes of the people that they cover. I think it was Mike O'Neill, who used to be editor of the New York *Daily News,* and I won't quote him exactly, because I can't, made the point that being in journalism doesn't free you from the other responsibilities or all the responsibilities that human beings ought to have. You ought not to feel like you can just become some sort of automaton that should not be required to think even once about the impact of what you do or the possible impact on the lives of innocent people, or maybe people who are not quite so innocent since most of us are a long way from being totally innocent, but people who are likely, because of what you do, to suffer much beyond any reasonable judgment of what would be appropriate. That's an elaboration of the point I was trying to get to with a secretary. Maybe I'll leave that out of the speech the next time.

QUESTION: You said something which occurred to me as being downright terrifying, and that is the fact that you said presidential decisions are defined or could be defined by decisions made without having access to all the options or information. That's terrifying to contemplate.

MR. POWELL: What I said and what I intended to say was that presidential decisions can be defined as decisions that are made with inadequate information to allow you to clearly choose among the options.

QUESTION: That's just as bad.

MR. POWELL: Well, bad or not, I think it is absolutely true. In the first place if there is a clear choice to be made, some Cabinet secretary is going to make the decision and take credit for it before it even gets to the White House, if it's that easy. But if you think back over the really tough decisions that a President has to make in almost any area— economics, nuclear weapons, defense in a general sense—you just don't know, and the call between A, B, C, D, or some mix of any two or three is very judgmental and extremely close.

Take one that this administration—the present administration— obviously has a completely different view from the one that was taken by the administration that I served in, whether we ought to build the B-1 bomber. That is a multi-billion dollar decision. It involves not only a lot of dollars but it's going to have a tremendous impact, for good or ill, on the nature of our national defense to the end of this century. It's in the top level of decision. That happened to be one I chose because that happened to be one that I had a chance to follow through and see every document of the President's and there were a ton of them. I guarantee you nobody knows with any absolute assurance whether or not the B-1 bomber is a good deal or not. It is a close call. I happen to think it's not; the man I served happened to think it's not. President Reagan thinks differently, and some very fine thoughtful people think differently. But if you went through it all and went through it all a dozen times, when you came out at the end, if you were a reasonably intelligent person, I think the first conclusion you would come to is that I'm not really sure that you can absolutely judge this one way or the other.

And you go right down the line: the size of tax cuts as opposed to tax increases as opposed to spending on this or that program depends upon some economists sitting around making projections about what the unemployment rate and inflation rate is going to be, not only when you start the budget process two or three years in the future which may depend upon whether or not you're going to have an oil crisis that doubles the price of oil in eight or ten months. In almost every instance that I witnessed I was glad I didn't have to make the decision because there are those sort of calls.

MR. TERHORST: I just want to add to what Jody said about the imperfect nature of the decision process when your man has to actually come down and say yes or no. This factor, I think, is worth thinking about, too, and it in no way diminishes Jody's answer. It is that we elect Presidents to make those hard decisions and take the responsibility for them even if he knows in his heart he doesn't know all the facts. That's where we separate Presidents from ordinary mortals, I guess.

QUESTION: Mr. Powell, I wonder if you would elaborate a few thoughts about whether after the Wtaergate incident the press coverage of the President and the political theater in general has been more detrimental or tended to look a little deeper and be more fair now?

MR. POWELL: I don't think there is any doubt that that decade of Vietnam and Watergate and all that was wrapped up in that changed forever the relationship between the White House and the press. It is as different now from what it was in 1950 as it is between 1850 and 1950, I would venture to say. Some of it was positive. I think the relationship was to some extent almost incestuous in some cases. On the whole I think there is a great deal about it, though, that has been unhealthy and that includes the persistent attitude on the part of people in government and people in the press that the relationship ought to be primarily adversarial—it is almost heresy to disagree with it and it has become a cliche, "Well, we all understand that's the relationship, that's fine, we all believe in that." I don't believe in it. I don't think that ought to be the primary way you define that relationship, and I think a good portion of the problems in the relationship are caused because we have come to look at it that way.

QUESTION: I was wondering if the new formal atmosphere in the press conferences is more valuable and responsible than the old way?

MR. THOMPSON: Under these auspices you can only give one answer.

MR. TERHORST: By formal you mean the formal nature of the present press conferences, you mean where reporters don't pop up and down like this and shout for attention, but Mr. Reagan picks them out? Well, Presidents always control every press conference. The amount of information that is elicited depends on two things: the reporter he recognizes who asks the question, obviously, and the nature of the question, and primarily the President's ability to answer that specific question. I think that's true whatever the format is. For myself I prefer the jump up kind of press conference because it is more natural. The problem with the existing format under President Reagan is that reporters now, it's fine to hold your hand up and be recognized, but it's now gotten so stylized that the President has beforehand a sheet of paper, with everybody having his assigned seat. There are names in all of those boxes, and that's why sometimes you find Mr. Reagan caught in a bind. He calls somebody's name out but the reporter isn't in that box and so he's calling a reporter by the wrong name. It has happened a couple of times. What happens when you formalize it is that you take really the liveliness out of the press conference. You make it a show piece, a set kind of theater which to my way of thinking is antithetical to a true press conference.

MR. THOMPSON: Last question, hopefully not on the press conference.

QUESTION: You said that you thought the press corps should not be adversarial. In my mind the press would not serve the public if it were not critical in its questions, if they and the President were not adversaries. If the President is not an adversary, if the press is not critical of what the President is doing, then how can we avoid Watergate or knowing of programs to which many people may object?

MR. POWELL: I figured somebody would jump on that. I did not object to the press beign critical in questioning. They obviously have to be that, certainly always questioning and critical when their judgment of the situation, as opposed to other extraneous factors, including the belief that you are not a good tough reporter unless you are adversarial and critical, dictates that they do that. I just think that idea of "well, it's an adversarial relationship" can be used to cover too great a multitude of sins. Call it adversarial if you want to, but if it is adversarial it certainly is not or ought not to be all-out war and there ought to be certain rules of the game by which you don't hit people below the knees on the kick-off or something like that to help the thing run a little more smoothly without doing such serious damage, not only to the people that are involved, but to the game or the process itself. I think that on many occasions journalists use that characterization of the relationship to justify behavior that on its own merits cannot be justified.

NARRATOR: We've had a veritable intellectual feast the last day and a half on this subject. That's what the Miller Center was created to do. We feel that our three guests have fulfilled the vision and objectives of the Miller Center to the highest imaginable possible degree. We do hope that you will continue to join us in this kind of an inquiry. We want to thank Mr. Powell, Mr. terHorst, and Mr. Reedy. We want to thank all of you for joining us in the Dome Room of the Rotunda.

THREE PRESS SECRETARIES ON THE PRESIDENCY AND THE PRESS

Jody Powell, George E. Reedy, Jerry terHorst

MR. THOMPSON: This session is the final effort of the Miller Center in the general area of the presidency and the press. You recall that some years ago now we formed a commission with which several of you met. We had a meeting with Jody Powell the day that there was a little conversation between the incoming and outgoing President about the time the two were scheduled for a certain appointment. So we thought we were close to history when we read the news account the next day. Others joined that commission, which was chaired by Governor Holton and Ray Scherer of RCA.

We simultaneously were undertaking four other ventures but they were slow in two instances in coming to fruition. Blaire French wrote a history of the presidential press conference which is available in paperback now and which has earned plaudits for the Miller Center from various places for being—this is to cast no aspersions on any of you in the profession—the best written account of the press conference which has yet been put forward. Maybe that's because Jim Young stood behind her as her guiding light as she wrote the book.

We had, six or eight months ago, about eight scholars here who wrote on particular Presidents and we published a little book called *Ten Presidents and the Press,* with Bob Donovan on Truman, George Juergens on Wilson and so on. And that little book has attracted considerable interest because under one cover it contains the impressions of some long-time scholars, long-time students of particular Presidents who in the volume wrote about their President's press relations. Bob Donovan said that he had collected a lot of material on Truman's relationship with the press which he never put in either of his volumes. But he did use it for this paper. So that is another venture.

The event just preceeding this meeting was an event with some of your friendly adversaries, members of the senior White House press corps, Helen Thomas, Frank Cormier, Jim Deakin and others who disclosed to us in considerable richness the various activities of Presidents and Presidents' staff in what was described as news management and cooption. Toward the end of the outline of the questions we gave you, questions six and seven in essence grow out of that discussion. But I thought we might work our way toward that subject rather than beginning with it and rather start with the substantive issues, although we can do anything you want in that regard. The agenda is yours to set as you see fit. You may want to start at some other point.

We cap the whole effort, then, with our discussion with three of you who have seen presidential-press relations from the press secretary's office and it seemed to us this was only fitting. We have fragments of some of your ideas in earlier publications, but it seemed to us that it would be very valuable if we could learn as much as possible from you and then try to complete, at least for now, our inquiry into the President and the press that has followed the course I described. David Clinton has been the director of special projects at the Miller Center and he and I have worked together on this effort, so I thought it would be appropriate if at least during most of the morning he could chair our discussions. But before we do that, do either you, Jody, or George or any of the rest of you have any thoughts about the order of our discussion? There's nothing sacred about the order of these questions. And maybe there's a more logical progression of thought than suggested by these questions. Maybe there's something missing, a question that hasn't been asked but is assumed.

1. What innovations did you make in the organization of the press secretary's office? What changes did you favor but find yourself unable to make? Are there any changes that you did not consider at the time, but, looking back on it, you now wish you had made? What are the single most important requirements for the success of a press secretary?

2. Other than his regular televised press conferences, what formats did the President use in his meetings with the press? Which were the most and least successful? What criteria were used in selecting one or the other? How did you prepare? What were the main problems?

3. Was there a discernible attitude on the part of the Washington press corps toward the President? Toward you and your office? Did this change over time?

4. What was the President's attitude toward the press? Did this change? What were the sources of his attitude and reasons for change?

5. Did you experience any problems in your role as the servant of these two masters, the President and the press? How did you reconcile these roles?

6. Members of the White House press corps have expressed the concern that Presidents attempt to coopt them through the use of threats and promises. Have you seen evidence to support this fear, in the administration you served or in others? Does the press exaggerate this fear? What instances do you recall when the press concern was valid?

7. Members of the press corps have discussed with us news management in various administrations. Can this concern be substantiated? How can the concern be eased? Is it an inevitable problem?

MR. REEDY: I'm not sure logic has got anything to do with any of it. I doubt if it matters, Ken. I think what's going to happen is the answer to a question is going to lead you to others. I don't care where you start, you're going to come out about the same end.

MR. CLINTON: I was wondering if you would like to follow the precedent of the presidential press conferences and have an opening statement to make before we begin to field the questions. Do either of you have some? The subject would be any thoughts, general thoughts that you might have, your experience as press secretary and the relationship between the President you served and the press.

MR. REEDY: I think there's one thing I would like to say which really helps me in the sense of laying a foundation for everything that I say afterwards. It will be brief. The principle problem I found in discussing the press secretary's job is the very widespread impression which is held by the press as well as by the public at large, that the press secretary is something like a minister of information in a parliamentary government. It is not sufficiently realized that the press secretary is there to speak for one man. The press secretary only had one vote for his job, the man that he's speaking for had an awful lot of votes. And it is not like a function of a parliamentary government where in effect, you have a collective Cabinet form of government and somebody is designated specifically within that Cabinet to determine what information shall be put out and what information should not be put out. One must start with the realization that that is what the press secretary is doing, period. He is speaking for the President. And of course he is making certain necessary arrangements to cover the President, because in the modern world it is not possible for the press to cover the President without the intervention of a rather high ranking official.

But so many of the things that the press secretary decides to do, the press will say: "The press secretary decided to do that." A press secretary may have decided to recommend something to the President, but the President back in the Oval Office is the one who decided what would be done, with one possible exception and that's Dwight D. Eisenhower. I think that President Eisenhower was so accustomed to the military staff and command system that he did to a great extent turn the press job over to Jim Hagerty, which is the reason why Hagerty's changes in the press office are probably the most lasting of any press secretary—not only because he was a very able man but because he had more elbow room. End of general statement.

MR. POWELL: Since you started on that, and that's a pretty good point to start on as a matter of fact, let me just add a couple of thoughts. I think what George says is right, but I also think that increasingly the White House, either through the press secretary or through someone else—and I might say parenthetically we tried it primarily through the press secretary, though I don't think that's the best way to do it—has tried primarily out of necessity to set up a coordinating function for information that does in fact behave in some ways like a government-wide information operation or parliamentary system or whatever. That has met with mixed success, and it has gone up and down even within a given administration. But I think that is a trend that is certainly going to continue because I don't think a President has much choice.

MR. REEDY: I agree with you, but I want to add one thing to it. I'm talking about the minister of information in a parliamentary form, where the minister has some choice, whereas you are speaking of a coordinating function in the federal government. The basic choice remains in the hands of the President. It is not in the hands of a Cabinet. That's a principal point that must be born in mind.

MR. CLINTON: Based on those statements and thoughts which you brought to the meeting, who would like to ask the first question?

QUESTION: When you say the man in the Oval Office makes the

decision, Mr. Reedy, what role do you have in suggesting to him when and where to have a press conference? It's his decision but wouldn't you be the one to recommend to him what date or what time of day, if it's going to be a.m. or p.m.?

MR. REEDY: Oh, of course. You've got to be very careful about something here. We live in a world where management functions are carefully defined, where there are structures in which everybody has a specific position. Each person knows who he or she reports to, who reports to him or her and that sort of thing. We tend to think of the White House in the same terms, when it's really not like that. Yes, the press secretary can recommend to the President. The President might or might not hold a press conference. My problem is that I usually had to figure out some kind of a gimmick to get Lyndon Johnson to hold a press conference. Some of you may remember the famous children's press conference where he had the press bring their children out on the South Lawn of the White House. The only reason it happened was that he had to have a press conference about that time and that was the only way I could get him to have a press conference. He loved gimmicks. One must realize that what power the press secretary has depends entirely upon his relationship with the President. If he has a very good relationship and is close to the President, he can get all sorts of things done. If he doesn't he can't get anything.

QUESTION: Why do you say he had to have a press conference? Is that your determination?

MR. REEDY: Well, my judgment as a professional journalist who understands that there is a certain point where the press has some questions and they had better get answers. There had been a number of developments in Vietnam and the President simply had to come up with some explanation. He was trying to get by through just sticking the whole thing over in the Defense Department. He was hoping that by so doing the onus would go on them rather than him. I could sense a mood that would lead to some really nasty stories if he did not appear and answer some questions. I couldn't get him to hold a press conference for sensible reasons. So I conned him into it with this idea of inviting the children of the press corps. There are times when even a poor answer is better than no answer, and that was one of those times. I think you would have agreed with me if you had been sitting where I was that it was question of professional judgment.

MR. POWELL: My problems to some extent were the opposite; I found myself having to come up with gimmicks to keep my boss from holding press conferences. Or stopping on the way to lunch to chit-chat with a reporter if he could see one. That for me was an even worse problem. I guess you have to live through both to decide which was the heavier cross to bear.

QUESTION: That wasn't because he wasn't very good at press conferences. Your restraints stem from a different consideration.

MR. POWELL: Yes. Again, it's a judgment call, but I thought and still do in retrospect that we probably talked too much. I think you can have too great a flow of information, particularly certain types of information from the government, and I think a President can involve himself too much publicly in everything that is happening within the government. And you really are dealing with to some extent two ends of the same problem. You can't, as George points out, get away with making the Cabinet officers in the departments carry all the heavy baggage for you. On the other hand, part of their job is to carry a significant portion of it and when you couple that with the fact that I think once everybody who has talked or written about this subject has made the point and it's very true that the whole thrust of coverage of the federal government is toward making every story a White House story if at all possible. If you can figure a way to get the story done standing at the front of the floodlit North Portico, then even if it relates to the Post Office Bureau or Department of whatever-it-is, then you've had a successful day and the networks have had a successful day.

QUESTION: How important is it for you to know what they know? Or isn't it a problem? Do you always know more than they know?

MR. REEDY: Know in what sense?

QUESTION: Knowing what the press corps is on to, how much they know about a particular subject.

MR. POWELL: Of the three or four rules, I would put that right at the top; right next to knowing the person you're dealing with would be knowing what they know and where they're coming from. Even if you know it, too, part of the question is how much of what you know do they know.

MR. REEDY: I can't imagine not knowing. I was a part of the press corps in Washington for so many years, the whole thing to me was second nature. They didn't even have to tell me; I usually knew what was on their minds because it would have been in my mind if I'd been in their position.

QUESTION: So you learned that just by instinct through experience and so forth? But are there techniques for knowing what they know that you develop along the way? I mean if you don't have the instinct? Maybe you all do.

MR. TERHORST: I'm not sure you can always know everything they know. I can think of a good many occasions when I was a reporter even on the Hill, or covering the White House, when I may have had a better handle on the story than the press office did at that point. I might have gotten it from a senator who had just come out of some important meeting in the White House and the press secretary perhaps hadn't even gotten a chance to see the President yet.

MR. REEDY: You're thinking in terms of individual facts, Jerry. I'm thinking of the overall thing. What they're after. Obviously you're never going to know everything.

MR. TERHORST: You cannot know what they're after.

MR. REEDY: I could usually figure that out.

MR. TERHORST: You could figure it out by the line of questions

MR. POWELL: A story came to mind that had to do with another aspect not long ago, the famous killer bees/neutron bomb story. When I first heard from Walter Pincus of the *Washington Post* about that thing I remember vaguely having read something I think in the late fifties about a neutron weapon when I think it was first discussed, and that was all I knew about it. I never heard anything about it again. And of course it turned into a major story and into a running international as well as domestic political controversy. You really are in a position of having to scramble just to catch up with where a guy like Pincus is who had worked on the Hill on that subject, knew it intimately, had been carrying a loaded pistol for that particular program for some time, just to the point that you know where he's off base and that sort of thing. It can be a problem in the specifics.

MR. REEDY: I think there's another factor you have to keep in mind. White House press coverage is somewhat stylized. At times it reminded me of some temple dances that I've seen in Bali. Where you have infrequent participation you will have some problems—Jody recalled to my mind when he mentioned Walter Pincus. Well, of course, he didn't normally cover the White House. A man like that might come in and give you a little bit of a problem, but otherwise I could walk in in the morning and I knew every single question I was going to be asked by Frank Cormier, Merriman Smith or by Sid Davis—you name them I knew them. One of the features of the White House is that things the President does, that are relatively unimportant if somebody else does them, become terribly important because the President does them and they should because the President is a symbol of the country. And that is why White House press coverage, at least in my day, tended to have a regularity to it. There were certain cycles you could anticipate. You knew when there were going to be ups and you knew when there were going to be downs. But if they introduced some new reporter in the White House, somebody who hadn't been there before, then you would have a period of two or three months in which some unexpected things could happen.

MR. POWELL: A thought occurred to me that may be something to which it may be good sense for somebody to look. Just as a theory, I would guess that the number, the amount of White House coverage that is now done by people not regularly assigned to the White House is much greater than it ever was. And, as George pointed out, the stinkers that you have to deal with are almost always or most often from those people and the bombs seldom explode at briefings. If Pincus has got a hot item on the neutron bomb, he's not going to ask the questions to build his first story at the briefing because everybody else is going to be on to it, too. He's going to do his first story, and then you'll have to deal with it in the briefing the next day. And you could predict what was going to go on in the briefing by reading the *Post* and the *Times* and the *Wall Street Journal* and the wires. That's it. You know what's coming.

QUESTION: So in a way they can't necessarily tip off what they know just in the meeting with you, because it tips off others as well.

MR. POWELL: Well, most of the good ones, it's not hard to get them to tell you and talk about it. They after all are looking for information. If a reporter just won't tell you and tries to play cute games, that's really pretty childish and bush, and you don't run into that very often except with the minority that are pretty childish and bush league about the thing. To them I'd say, "Look, I need to figure out what going on here myself; why don't you come see me in three hours and maybe I'll be able to help you with the thing, or if not, I'll get some people in here that can, but I don't know a thing about it right now."

QUESTION: Would you say a little bit more about the other side of that and that is knowing what you know, that is knowing what's going on in the White House and what's happening there that's going to make the news. How do you keep on top of all that? What kind of structure do you develop? And does it differ among the three of you in your experiences in the White House?

MR. REEDY: The President makes news. There are an awful lot of White House assistants that have some idea that they make it. They don't. They just get in the papers sometimes. That's how Tommy Corcoran disappeared from the White House. The President makes news.

MR. POWELL: But those other guys can sure as hell make problems, which in terms of having to deal with them amount to the same, whether it's news or not.

MR. REEDY: You see, if it doesn't come from the President it's not a story as far as I'm concerned.

MR. TERHORST: Quite often I've found that you're faced with a problem, the elite problem. If you have a couple of good friends in the White House you can kind of get a feeling from the meetings what they're going to go to that day what the issues may well be. And if you can possibly ferret out with just a hint or two from them or if nothing else saying, "Look, if I went in and asked George Reedy or Jody Powell, how far off base would I be?" Well, if he's a friend of yours he might say, "Might be worth trying." Or if he'd say, "Oh, I don't think you'll get anything," then I'd know maybe either I'm on the wrong track or it hasn't jelled yet. But acting as press secretary, I have found quite often that I would sometimes get questions that hadn't come out of the Oval Office and didn't relate to anything the President was doing but something that the President was suspected of being interested in doing or was about to do. Consequently I'd say well, we'll talk about that when we're ready, or I can't comment on it now or, you know, you have to push those things aside because it hadn't come from the President.

MR. REEDY: I think we have to make a distinction here. If you mean what kind of a setup does one have to have to get news to the press, that's one thing. That's not the problem. The problem is the problems that's been outlined both by Jody and by Jerry, the fact that you will have White House assistants who are very, very happy to get some stuff going.

MR. POWELL: And three or four levels down in the major departments, too. That can generate, given the proper issue, a nice little squabble to have to deal with.

MR. REEDY: I'm making a distinction so I want to get back to the statement I opened with. You are not there to feed news to the press. You are there to speak for the President. And obviously you can't speak for the President without giving the press a lot of news, but that's not basically your purpose. Again, if you had a minister of information in a parliamentary government, that minister of information would have to have some kind of machine whereby he could circulate the entire government to find out what's going on. But what the White House press secretary needs to know is what the President's thinking.

QUESTION: I meant something a little bit different from either of the distinctions you made but it's related to the point that you make that you're working for the President and the President makes the news. But the presidency is obviously not just a single individual; it's an institution and it's epitomized by the White House and the operation within the White House. Therefore, presumably what's happening within the White House is related to what the President is and the news that he's going to make so that it comes to be an extension of him and I would guess that it's important for you to keep on top of what kind of issue and policy generation is going on there as a backdrop to how the President is going to make a decision.

MR. REEDY: Don't lean too heavily on that. Again, I said at the start, we're so accustomed to an organizational world which has been analyzed by all the motivational behavioral scientists that we tend to think of the White House in the same terms. The President does what he wants to do. Obviously there are certain restraints upon him because we must assume that this is a man of intelligence. He does have some ties to the past. But it's amazing how quickly a President can cut across, if he wishes, all of the advice, all of the so-called decisionmaking apparatus. I have participated in more studies of the decisionmaking processes of the White House and I don't think any of them, in terms of the White House, are worth the paper they're written on. What they've gotten is a study on the decisionmaking processes of a particular President, whereas decisionmaking can vary tremendously from President to President. I think Eisenhower was probably the closest model to a well organized President, but that was closer to the military model than it was to the modern management structures.

MR. TERHORST: They will vary, too, I would suggest, depending on the personality of the President, the way he came to office, the style in which he likes to operate as a human being, and also the internal relationships he has with members of his Cabinet. Is he truly the boss of that Cabinet or has he got a couple of mavericks in the Cabinet that he really has no choice but to keep right now but would just as soon get rid of as soon as he could? And then also the question of whether he has any particularly ambitious people on his White House staff. And then beyond that what are his relationships with Congress? Is he really in charge of his party on the Hill or is the party on the Hill not under his thumb?

MR. REEDY: I don't think there has ever been anybody in charge of their party on the Hill.

MR. TERHORST: Well, the party leader may reach a point where he doesn't hesitate to defend the man in the White House.

MR. REEDY: Well, for the first couple of years a President can get almost anything he wants out of the Congress. But again, let me go back to another point. You have to realize that the distinction of the presidency, and any other position you can think of within the United States, is that the presidency is a position of ultimate responsibility. Everybody says that but I don't think the whole force of the remark has sunk home. This is not the president of General Motors or General Electric. He's not even the presiding bishop of the Episcopal church who has some collegiality he must rely on. The President is the ultimate end. And as Harry Truman demonstrated, boy, he could fire. He could fire no matter how much trouble it was going to cause. He bounced Wallace, he bounced MacArthur; it may not have been a prudent thing for him to have done and Presidents do a lot of things that aren't very prudent. But the difference is they can do things that aren't very prudent.

MR. THOMPSON: I wonder if we could do what we've done in the oral history project for just a moment. When each of you have come in, we have always asked what ideas did you bring to the office and what changes in your attitude occurred as you worked in it? We had a little bit of that in mind with the first question about innovations, changes. Are there any changes that you did not consider at the time but looking back you wish you had made? If we could talk for just a moment about this it would be helpful. What did you think about the office when you came in? What did you do? What happened that changed your mind, if at all? And what changes occur to you now?

MR. POWELL: Can I say one thing on this last topic, that I hope will add something? What George says is true, that your ultimate and primary responsibility is to speak for the President. But that doesn't mean that you can ignore things that crop up that haven't gotten to the President yet and maybe never will, certainly may not for a week or two. Because the intensity of the focus these days is such that if you don't get on top of some of these things early, then by the time it gets to the President the thing is so skewed that in effect his decisionmaking options are limited. As George says, the President can decide what he wants to do. But deciding to go out and beat your head up against a brick wall is not exactly the way you want to put it. You don't want to leave the guy that way any more frequently than you have to. I found at least that if I didn't get myself involved to some extent in a story that was moving toward the White House early that I had a time dealing with it after it got there because I didn't understand, in some cases, the substance of the matter, in other cases, which was as important if not more important, the political process that was involved, who was on what side within the administration, what arguments were being made internally, who was liable to take off on this tangent or the other. If something is already in the Congress, it's even worse because you've got players up there. So you do have to have some sort of early warning system, and you do need people working for you that can, as these things pop up and start moving your way, sometimes in a big hurry, begin to collect the information, identify the players, get you ready and, in some cases, put you in a position to try to at least keep the thing reasonably close to the middle of the track so that by the time it comes to the President all the arguments have not been made on just one side. Just because a certain element or faction within the administration holding a particular point of view is better at dealing with the press than another does not necessarily mean that their policy advice to the President is always the best. And in fact I would almost be willing to posit a rule that it's probably exactly the opposite. And with any given administration those people who are most adept at advancing their views and limiting the President's options in dealing with the press are also most likely to give the President bum advice. And it may be because they have found that the weakness of their arguments and their lack of homework can only be compensated for by building the case early.

MR. THOMPSON: One of the things that came up all through the hearings on our press commission report was how do you prepare for this kind of thing? Somebody said you prepare to be a secretary in a key department by being stuck in a room with fifty thousand white mice and see what you would do with them. But how do you prepare for this early warning process and the other things? Is it by being a newsman? Ninety percent of the people we talked to said that a press secretary *had* to have been a newsman. Is it political experience, academic experience, thinking about the job? What is it?

MR. REEDY: I'm in the ten percent bracket.

QUESTION: You raised an interesting question which was that you could tell what was happening because you worked around Washington for so long and been a newspaper man. You could anticipate what the press was thinking. Admittedly, Richard Nixon didn't have a very good relationship with the press to begin with, but would this relationship have been any better if he had not had a man from Disneyland as his press secretary who had no experience?

MR. REEDY: It wouldn't have made any difference.

MR. TERHORST: He had press people. Jerry Warren, for example, an excellent newsman, a real professional on his staff as the number two man. And Warren was almost completely ineffectual in stopping what you're talking about. Herb Klein is another who was there. At the outset he was fine but toward the end of his term, he knew when it was time for him to go because he no longer had any clout.

QUESTION: Then Jody came in. As I recollect, Jody, you weren't even a newspaperman down in Georgia, were you? In other words, you had no press experience and yet came away from that zoo with a pretty good reputation as a press secretary.

MR. REEDY: It's not necessary. What is necessary—there's only one thing that's really necessary—is to have a President's confidence. Everything else is secondary. The difficulty is that it is not a public relations job, really. I do not despise public relations. I have no illusions there will not be public relations in the White House. There will. But the press secretary's job is that of a contact for the press in both directions.

QUESTION: How many of those implications did you fully understand when you came to the press secretary's job and how much was a learning process while you were in it?

MR. REEDY: I understood most of them before I got the job and that is why I didn't want it. They hauled me out of a hospital bed and slammed me into it. But I understood it fairly well.

MR. TERHORST: I would have to say it was the same with me because I had covered the White House for sixteen years before Ford tapped me. So I had a pretty good idea how the game is played. Everything was the stylized ritual that George referred to, even to my role in it or alongside of it—because I was not, obviously a wire service person or a network person, what we call the "regulars" among on the press corps, but only represented one paper, and not even a paper that was well read in Washington.

But to get back to your question of what you would do, how you prepared for this sort of thing, and what changes you came in with that you wanted to make, that you could see. The first thing I obviously had to do, I thought I had to do, because that's what the President wanted done—and I could see he was on the right track—was help him make a sharp break between himself and Richard Nixon. Not in terms of party affiliation obviously, or in terms of who his friends were, because they were mutual. You couldn't separate Nixon Republicans in those days from Jerry Ford Republicans or any other Republicans because if you weren't a Nixon Republican, what were you? Nixon had been vice president and President before Jerry Ford came on for six years. So it wasn't a case of dividing it up that way.

But Ford definitely wanted to make a change himself, and in the press area he entrusted me and charged me with making the changes that would create a new climate. So the first thing I decided to do was to consolidate the press operation under the press secretary. The

President made it easier because at the outset he had decided he wanted to run a kind of collegial staff—I would have authority to go in and talk to him without having to go through the chief of staff. As you know, under the Nixon presidency everybody went in either through Haldeman and then through Al Haig. Al Haig even decided what you might say to the President about certain issues, in some cases, if he had his way. So Ford didn't want that. He wanted to use what was euphemistically called the "spokes of the wheel," where he was at the center of the hub and everybody who had something worth saying *and* had a senior staff position had a right to talk to him. That's a great theory, but not a good way to run the White House, as it turns out in the long run, because the hub can't keep track of what the spokes around him are doing.

In doing that, the first thing I did was to eliminate the autonomy and independence of what was called the Office of Communication which was over in the Executive Office Building (EOB) and had been started by Herb Klein through Richard Nixon and had continued on. At the point I took over it had become practically an adjunct for the Nixon defense on Watergate. It was cocktails with Clausen every night at five after the latest briefing by Jaworski, or by one of the special prosecutors or one of the defense lawyers for the President. This was to feed certain information to reporters the White House was trying to use or [information] that the Nixon White House was trying to get out. It didn't report to Ron Zeigler at all. In fact it reported to Al Haig. With the President's permission, I consolidated that office and told a number of those people there, look, I'm not going to push you out but let's say you have thirty days to find another job and I won't say anything about it until you get your other job. Because the guard had changed it was time for them to look elsewhere. A few of them I tried to place. George Bush was then chairman of the party and I can recall a couple of times calling him and saying we've got some pretty good political talent over here in EOB. Maybe you can use them in the party structure because that's where they belong; they don't belong over here at the White House under the kind of operation I'm trying to set up. I don't think he took any of them, so they all had to go out and look for other work, as it were. But some of them didn't want to look for other work. They spent an enormous amount of time going around the back door trying to persuade Al Haig that I was persecuting them, trying to get rid of them and they had done their job and therefore they thought they should hang on with the Ford White House. But in the end I had my way because I had the President with me. If he hadn't been with me, I wouldn't have succeeded.

Also up to that point the White House had maintained a terribly tight control over who should be on *Meet the Press, Face the Nation, Issues and Answers,* and those kinds of talk shows—people in the government such as Cabinet secretaries down to the chief White House staff people. I frankly got a little bored with getting called, say, on Thursday by some Cabinet secretary wanting to know if it was all right with me if he appeared on such and such a show. The control was very tight, tighter than I had thought it was as a reporter. The President said, if they're going to stay in the Cabinet they're going to have to learn to make those decisions themselves—which was fine with me, too, because it just eliminated a lot of work load. So I no longer played traffic cop in that sort of thing.

There's a question here: what would I undo. I would not have, I think, given up that control quite as completely. Perhaps I would if I had come in at a different time and if there wasn't such a need to try to create a new climate for Jerry Ford. I think I would have kept some reins on that [traffic] because, even though I was there very briefly, before the end of my stint it was clear that some Cabinet people were already taking advantage of the opportunity not to check in with the White House on what they were going to say on *Face the Nation* or *Meet the Press*. The Monday briefings were getting to be a pain in the neck for the President if not for me.

So those are a couple of structural things that I set out to accomplish. I really felt, and still feel, it's a shame that, for some reason or other, there is a need for this kind of control, that there has to be some sort of top-level monitoring by the White House on who goes on the shows and what is going to be said or what's not going to be said: Maybe the President could preserve his options a little better when questions come up about issues that are only in a stage of ferment and not really at the decision point.

MR. REEDY: I'd like to add one thing and that is that what Jerry is saying brings home very closely to me how different Presidents are. There was no problem with access to Lyndon Johnson. In fact one of the problems was almost anybody could walk in and see him as long as they walked in the right way. On the other hand, however, there was an extraordinarily tight control over every Cabinet officer and everybody else, but it was exercised by Lyndon Baines Johnson. It was not exercised by his assistant.

MR. POWELL: We established to some extent the—control is perhaps too strong a word—but at least having the Cabinet members and the senior staff check with the press office. And also the understanding, which was sometimes honored more in the breech, that if we asked them to make an appearance—I mean that's really the other side of it—that these people are a resource for the President, and if you need them to do a job for you on *Meet the Press* or you name it, they ought to be willing to do it. If you want them to step aside and say no so you can place someone else, they ought to be willing to do it. And if you want them to do *Face The Nation* because *Face The Nation* has missed big Cabinet names the past five weeks and they're getting a little upset about it, you need to give them somebody to quiet them down; they ought to be willing to do that, too.

MR. TERHORST: We did that sort of operation.

MR. POWELL: Yes, you want to tread a thin line. You want those people that schedule these programs to know that you can do it if you really want to. On the other hand, you don't want them to think that you're just doing it all the time so that you're always responsible for every decision. You need to have a stronger hand than you show so that when you want to move things around you can do it.

QUESTION: I have a question about the press secretary's job or about your views about this matter outside of just dealing with the press, the question of publicizing the President's point of view or the administration's point of view outside an interview situation, either in briefing or in press conference. I take it this is one of the things that Herb Klein was doing early in the Nixon years before it turned into a Watergate defense operation. Is that an important responsibility of the press secretary and the press secretary's office in your experience or as you see it? That is, his doing things besides dealing with the press and publicizing an administration viewpoint or a presidential viewpoint other than through interviews with the press?

MR. POWELL: You mean presidential interviews with . . .

QUESTION: Either yours or the President or a press conference format. Publicity for the President's viewpoints other than that communicated through interview situations with people of the press. You're thinking about perhaps speech making or position papers, release of documents?

MR. REEDY: You mean a public relations operation? Is that what you mean, a public relations operation? It's up to the President. It'll be done by somebody.

QUESTION: Is that part of the press secretary's job?

MR. POWELL: It could be, but not necessarily. I mean different Presidents have different views. The President I worked for didn't ever think five minutes about telling so and so to go and do a backgrounder on this or we need to get Brzezinski to do this and so on. He probably still hasn't thought five minutes about it.

MR. TERHORST:Let me give you an idea of how it worked on one issue. Early on in Ford's term, I think it was only the second week, he had, of course, to face the task of picking a vice president. And he was, as you might expect, bombarded with suggestions from everybody under the sun who thought he had a right to tell the President who would make a good choice or who should be his choice. The President wasn't adverse to that. He knew in the back of his mind he was going to make the choice anyway, so the more people that got into the act and felt part of it would feel better afterward. This was a participatory event. He was smart enough to know this would be good for all hands. On the other hand, he wasn't going to let it get out of his grasp, either.

But there were times in those first couple of weeks, when that appeared to be the case, by just the sheer number of stories that were popping up in the *New York Times* and the *Los Angeles Times* and the *Washington Post* and the *Washington Star* and in the wires about who was coming in to see the President. Mel Laird was a great guy but had a propensity for sitting in his office at Reader's Digest and propounding publicly to a handful of selected correspondents what he had told Jerry Ford and what he was pretty sure his good old friend Jerry Ford was going to do. After about a week or so of that Ford began to get just a little—I guess "irritated" would be a pleasant word to use. Yet he didn't want to call Mel Laird down and didn't want him to go public with it. So he delegated me and another chap—I guess I'd better not mention him because I never have—to ask Mel Laird to come in and explain the problem to him, which we did. And he (Laird) was very apologetic. He said, gee whiz, I didn't realize I was causing so much trouble, and do you want me to see the President? At some point he (Laird) did go and see the President and told the President some of our concerns. Jerry Ford said, well, as a matter of fact, that's right, I am getting very upset about this.

That's one way. Perhaps, that partly answers the question you raised. Maybe that's P.R. that I was engaged in, but it was necessary at least not to let the image get out across the country that Jerry Ford was just sitting there waiting for somebody to take a vote to tell him who was going to be the vice president. Because he knew right from the beginning that he wanted Nelson Rockefeller and he was just trying to find a way to make it happen so that everybody in the party would swallow it without screaming.

QUESTION: I was trying to see if you want to go further in this. The question was inspired or brought to mind by Jody's comment about asking people on the Cabinet to go out and explain something, when they had an interview opportunity or an opportunity to be on a talk show. My question was, does the press secretary's job go beyond that, beyond the means of just placing people to get photo opportunities and talk opportunities, but doing something by the way of organized effort?

MR. POWELL: That's got to be done.

QUESTION: To get a presidential viewpoint across other than in the limitations of the infrequently held press conference.

MR. POWELL: That's got to be done. Whether the press secretary should be the person to do it is a good question. I'm inclined to think that he probably should be, but he can't because I tried to do it and I don't think I was able to devote enough time to it. On the other hand, the press secretary has got to have a good hand in that operation or you get at cross purposes. The one that comes immediately to mind to me was the fight over the Panama Canal treaties. Maybe it wasn't public relations; if it wasn't, it was close to it. You had literally hundreds of people involved in that. And you're dealing not only with *Meet the Press* and those shows but "Good Morning Idaho" and "Hello Atlanta" and "Talk Radio" and Lord knows what all else. Well, that takes a lot of coordination. You've got to free the people up. You've got to tell them where to go. You've got to make sure that they say what they're supposed to say when they get there and so forth. There's no doubt in my mind, I can say this without being immodest since I wasn't really in charge of it, that those treaties would never have been approved if it had not been for a lot of other things, but for that sort of operation, too. You really saw a rather dramatic movement in public opinion in the course of just six months on that issue.

MR. REEDY: But you've got to get back to something, though. I think you have to realize that normal concepts of what organization is do not apply to the White House. In other words, when you say is it within the responsibility of the press secretary, that depends on what the President wants done. The operation that Jerry terHorst described, for example, Lyndon Johnson would have called in Abe Fortas to do it or he might have reached out and gotten Clark Clifford or somebody of that nature.

The titles in the White House can be very misleading. Under Jack Kennedy the principal occupation of the general counsel of the White House was writing speeches. Under Lyndon Baines Johnson the principal occupation of the general counsel was liaison with the black community. I don't know when either one of them actually engaged in any kind of general counselling to the White House. There are only three titles in the White House you can be sure of: the press secretary, because he has to have contact with the press; the advisor of the national security council because he has to have contact with the agencies; and the chief butler.

QUESTION: My question was is it an important part in what you consider the press secretary's job to organize presentations of the President's viewpoint? Jody said yes, but he can't handle it all.

MR. POWELL: That's an important job.

MR. REEDY: You're going to do it but who cares?

MR. POWELL: Yes, and the press secretary certainly has to play a role in it.

QUESTION: Listening to some of your discussion and looking back over most of the modern presidencies, it seems that a President's relationship with the press has fallen into a regular cycle or a kind of boom and bust cycle, starting off beautifully with the honeymoon year and then moving into a more mixed and increasingly negative coverage leading to the third year blues and finally to a very cynical election year coverage. First of all, I'd be interested in knowing your view about whether or not that cycle, as outsiders perceive it, is really accurate or whether it's oversimplified? And secondly, is there anything that the press secretary and the press secretary's office can do in the modern presidency to break that cycle, or is it really beyond the scope of what the press secretary does or even beyond the public relations tools at a President's command?

MR. REEDY: You're wrong about the modern presidency. I can take you all the way back to George Washington and you're going to find the same thing happened. There's only been two exceptions—Gerald Ford and that was mostly because he had not been elected. You know, the election process is a sanctification process as well as a selection process. I think it makes a difference. The other is William Henry Harrison who died a month after he took over the job. But you can go all the way back to George Washington. I did a rather careful study of this and what you are describing, I would describe differently myself. What you are doing is giving a certain perception of certain events that are almost as automatic as the return of the swallows to Capistrano. And I think it's inherent within the very nature of the American government. I don't think you can really change it unless you start playing games with the Constitution.

The day after a President is elected you can't find anybody who voted against him. And that's not because they're being insincere or sycophantic; it's just the sudden realization: my God, he's our President for four years. You get one year—sometimes more than that, depending upon the President—in which what journalists are really concentrating on is the man himself. Newspapermen are just like any other Americans; they want the President to succeed, at least during the first year. But then toward the end of that year what you start getting is coverage of what he's doing. And you cannot do anything in this world without dividing people. The old Greek saying is everytime you do somebody a favor you make nineteen enemies and one ingrate, which is pretty much the way the world works. And once he starts becoming the active leader of the government, what is going to follow is a lot of rough and tumble coverage which he is going to interpret as being directed against him, but actually it's nothing but rough and tumble coverage. I don't think the press is anti-President. I think what is happening is the press reports the political realities of times and in the political realities of the times there are an awful lot of people that are anti-President and they're going to be reported.

QUESTION: Apropos of that, I was fascinated by a statistic this morning in the *Times Dispatch* from George Gallup talking about the President's second year popularity, the average percentage. For the first two years, Reagan's average was forty-six, I believe it was, and Jimmy Carter's was forty-seven. Jack Kennedy's was seventy-two. And that's a pretty big fall-off in twenty years.

MR. REEDY: You're trying to read a very complex statistic that the pollsters have never been very happy with, the presidential popularity rating. Precisely what does it mean? Does this really register the popularity of the President or does it register what the people think about their country? Don't forget at the time that Jack Kennedy was President you had a country that had a relatively coherent consensus. That is something that has fallen away badly since Lyndon Johnson, between Vietnam and Watergate and other things. I think today that you're in one of the periods of American history that's very much like the period from 1848 to 1860 in which there is no coherent consensus. I do not believe that anybody could get a really high rating today. I believe that Reagan's rating is phenomenally high myself.

MR. POWELL: I agree with what you say completely. Ten of those twenty years had a profound effect on everything.

MR. THOMPSON: Could we leave question one with a subordinate question; is there anything any of you would change looking back on what you did in the office that you left?

MR. REEDY: I would have said no.

MR. POWELL: I would have tried to do less. And do some things that I brought into the press office that I thought I could have sitting there to fiddle with when I felt like it. And I found out that doesn't work. Like speech writing, for example. If it's there you're going to get blamed. You're going to have to jump into it when you least want to.

MR. REEDY: I would like to add one other thought, though, which I think is apropos. There really is only one important thing about the press office and that is that it be believed. The integrity of the press office is absolutely essential. When the press secretary does start getting into other fields then what happens is that the press office loses some of its believability. When a press secretary says yes, the press must believe him.

MR. POWELL: Necessary but not sufficient.

QUESTION: Does that mean that you should always separate the Rafshoonery types of functions that the new White House has been acquiring from the press secretary's office?

MR. REEDY: Well, what you should do and what will be done are two different things. You know, if wishes were horses, beggars could ride. Yes, I think it would probably be very useful to the President if the press office could be set up on a separate basis, but no President is going to do it. Lyndon Johnson thought of the press office as a super public relations job. He thought Charlie Michelson had elected Roosevelt. Charlie Michelson wasn't the press secretary but he was publicity director for the Democratic National Committee. He thought Pierre Salinger had elected Jack Kennedy. I don't know who he thought elected Harry Truman. What he was doing was forcing public relations gestures upon the press office. Consequently, I may be oversensitive to it, but I think Lyndon Johnson hurt himself very badly by pushing so many of these crusades of his into the press office.

MR. POWELL: Let me make a point on the other side of it, not to argue but just to put the considerations on the table. First of all, even if I think just in terms of what a person can do, even if you separate it, the President is still going to get hung with it if it's done badly. And the credibility attaches itself not just to the press office but to the White House generally. If generally you are doing things that are not credible, if you're saying things that prove not to be true, in the end the White House and the President get a questionable reputation. The other consideration is that if you stick that thing off to one side too much you run the danger of it being run by public relations type operatives in the less complimentary sense of the word, and they are much more likely to get themselves involved in foolishness than if the people who have some line responsibility and have to suffer the consequences of their behavior have a hand in it.

MR. REEDY: I think that, Jody, both of us said the same thing: the test is going to be how the President does it.

MR. TERHORST: It goes back again to who the President is and the time in which, the atmosphere in which he's governing and what the immediate antecedents were, and I have to look at that hard every time, of course, because of the way Jerry Ford came into power. There are always people in the White House staff who believe that the press office is not serving the President well and that, for some reason or other, things are falling between the crack. If the press office were doing it right, this wouldn't happen. The President hears static from people on the staff or from people in the government or from friends of the party or elsewhere. He hears it and so it weighs on his mind. And right there, he's got to decide whether he believes in his press secretary or doesn't. He has to have some sort of faith in what the man can do. So, as Jody says, sometimes these people take it on their own to fulfill some kind of a P.R. or propaganda type operation to sell a certain viewpoint. And if it's not done well or if it's not done credibly, the press office then has to live with the fallout. So you end up getting it anyway. You end up being stuck with the problem even if you aren't actually part of it.

To get back to what George says, the "believability" of that office really is so important. That was really what did Ron Ziegler in; nobody believed him any more. Even the most careful members of the press corps, who usually are the wire service reporters who are there day in and day out, were asking Ron Ziegler, "Ron, when's the last time you saw the President?" They knew he was getting almost everything he had to say from somebody else, usually Al Haig. Everything he was saying, even before he said his famous "inoperative" phrase, was already being disbelieved. So credibility is terribly important. And actually that was one of the basic reasons why I resigned after the pardon. I could see that suddenly my job no longer was credible to the press, given the nature of the way the pardon came out. It was a surprise: On a Sunday morning the American people were told about it by a President who up to that point publicly was maintaining the position that when this issue comes before me, if the special prosecutor makes an announcement, then I will decide it. So that was part of the reason why I left. I felt, as I told him, that I could not defend the pardon in a credible way. I didn't believe in it personally as well, which was the second reason.

QUESTION: That makes an important point though for, press secretaries. It's awfully hard for the press secretary to separate himself from the credibility of the President. In Ziegler's case, he was not serving a credible President.

MR. POWELL: Nobody could have done Ziegler's job well. You

either end up being a liar, or you end up leaving in a job like that. There's no way to win.

MR. REEDY: I think one thing's being illustrated here is what a tremendous difference the personality of the President makes. I think that both Jody and Jerry are talking about public relations in a somewhat different sense than I am because Lyndon Johnson was a man whose idea of public relations was that of Ringling Brothers and Barnum and Bailey. In other words, he wanted to have the world's tallest midget and the world's shortest giant. He wanted the drums beat and the bugles blown. And that's one of the reasons, not the only one, why Johnson and I finally came to the parting of the ways. He once explained to me that the job of the press secretary was to figure out how to get pictures in the paper and to figure out stories to get the President's name in the paper and he said I wasn't imaginative because I didn't look upon it that way. I'll admit my imagination was not enough to keep me awake nights trying to figure out how to get the President's name in the newspaper. How to keep it out, was a more relevant problem to me.

MR. POWELL: That's what you lay awake at night worrying about.

MR. THOMPSON: We included this second question because all through the discussions on the press conference, most of you or all of you kept saying, don't equate the President's communication with the press conference. So we've asked the question in the agenda we've drawn up. What are the other formats the President can use to advance his viewpoint? Which work and which don't work and is there anything one can say in general or does this simply depend upon the individual President? We had in mind town meetings, radio speeches, all the things that enter into play. Is it true that Reagan is good at some things and he ought to do only those? And that Carter was good at some things and he ought to do only those? Or is it true that the circumstances and problems at any given moment call for different formats? How did you decide? Did you make mistakes or what would you do differently in that area?

MR. POWELL: I think one thing to be said is you have to understand the press will never feel that they have enough access to the President. They don't even feel they have enough access to the press secretary much less the President. And no matter what you do, if they could follow him into the shower every day, and if you don't think Helen Thomas would do that and I say that as a compliment actually, she would. And several others, too. So you're always going to have that sort of problem to deal with. Beyond that, the identity of the

President as to who he is and what he's like is the controlling factor. You can't completely eliminate the press conference, for example, if he's not good at press conferences. You can't eliminate speeches if he's not good at speeches, but you can certainly de-emphasize them.

QUESTION: Could I ask something on that? Two footnotes to history here. First, Jerry, you were talking about changing Ford's image, of giving him a favorable image. Were you the man responsible for the President doing his own English muffins?

MR. TERHORST: Well, I guess I had a hand in getting the story out. That story really wasn't anything we created. As you recall the first few days of the presidency while the White House and the Oval Office were being renovated after Nixon and the Nixon files and everything else were being removed, Jerry Ford pretty much operated for a couple of days out of his house in Alexandria. They were taking pictures of him going to the door in his robe, reaching out and getting the paper and this sort of thing. It was a new look at a President, obviously. It hadn't happened before. And it was well known that he always did make his breakfast there, so the question sort of sprung from that. Was he still doing his own toast and his muffins? It was no secret either that Mrs. Ford was a late sleeper and Jerry Ford was an early riser and so, yes, he did. Then the next question of course, could they get a picture? Well, I thought that was a good idea; I didn't plan it myself. It came right out of the press corps.

QUESTION: My question to you, Jody, is, did you have anything whatsoever to do with President Carter's decision to get out of the car on inauguration day and walk down Pennsylvania Avenue?

MR. POWELL: No. But it wasn't spontaneous; it didn't happen at that moment. He thought of it. He decided to do it and he checked with the Secret Service to make sure it could be done. He told me afterwards that that was what he was going to do and that if it got out ahead of time he couldn't do it.

MR. REEDY: I think that actually the most successful means of communication Lyndon Johnson had were symbolic. I think one of the best things that President Carter ever did, too, was that walk down Pennsylvania Avenue. I thought that was masterful. The next thing that I thought was masterful was that energy speech in front of the fireplace. Johnson, for example, was great at such things as walking through the White House snapping off the lights. Then it leaked out that he was walking through the White House snapping off the lights and every businessman in the country said, "Ah ha, a man that understands the value of the dollar." He was awfully good at that. I think that when he charged through a crowd shaking hands, that was terribly effective. His most ineffective things were the informal meetings he held with the press which were absolutely God awful, because he did not understand newspapermen—he did not know what they were after. He abolished the press pool aboard Air Force One, the reason being that he thought the reporters were just there to spy, to see what stories they could sneak out and that if somebody wasn't talking to them every minute they were going to write nasty stories. For once the press got tired of seeing the President because all those poor men wanted was to sit there and have a quiet drink and relax. The only reason the pool existed was because Eisenhower's plane sat down in a cow pasture in Tennessee once and some of the local press who did not understand the White House wrote some stories that caused some problems for Jim Hagerty. Jim Hagerty instituted the press pool. And Johnson abolished it. He was really rather good at press conferences. But whenever he'd get a reporter in informally all by himself, it would be terrible. He thought that everybody spent all their time working at their job. Every time he saw a lawyer he thought the lawyer was looking for an ambulance to chase. Every time he saw a doctor he thought the doctor was looking for a broken ankle. Every time he saw a newspaperman he thought the newspaperman was looking for stories. He did not know when to relax.

MR. POWELL: Wasn't half dumb, was he? He understood doctors, lawyers and newspapermen.

MR. REEDY: It's funny to be amused by it, but no living human being lives that way, except Lyndon Johnson.

MR. TERHORST: But at some point he did reinstate the pool because I can recall being on a good many trips with the pool.

MR. REEDY: Yes, it became too ridiculous. But he didn't reinstate it until he'd had his nose pretty bloody as a result of a plane being late, or something like that, and nobody was around to report on it. And also once he had a big trip over flood scenes in Missouri and nobody there to take pictures of him looking sympathetically out the window. The press pool got back.

MR. POWELL: Let me raise a question for you two, because it was what I started to say before and I forgot my second point while making the first point. The other point I was going to make is about access; what you said just reminded me of it. One of the things I always had a hard time keeping in my mind, what I believed to be true, is that basically the public doesn't give a damn about these questions of access, and that if you are determined to do it, for the most part, the press itself is also a bit of a paper tiger on these access questions. They'll scream and moan and cry. But if it's done effectively, you can get away, within limits, with just about anything. I would keep reminding myself of that on a Saturday morning and then by Tuesday I had forgotten it again. I think that President Reagan has shown with his operation that these guys and women are a little bit paper tigers when they scream and shout about this, but in the end they have to deal with what they got.

MR. REEDY: As long as you do not really interfere with the kind of coverage they should be getting, then what happens is not that the public is going to get sympathetic with the press, they aren't. But the President can reach a point where a number of things that he wants to get out won't get out.

MR. POWELL: If they ever get you down, if once you start dragging a leg and shedding a little blood, then retribution can be extracted.

MR. REEDY: I agree with you, Jody. I don't think the public could care less. The only people that are really interested in journalistic problems are journalists.

QUESTION: The people who were here played the photo opportunity thing to a maximum. They said they thought there was a public reaction against Reagan's use of the photo opportunities to an excessive degree. You wouldn't agree that the public cared at all about that?

MR. TERHORST: I don't think the man on the street ever knows whether he is being more accessible—or less.

MR. REEDY: In Walski's Tavern on the south side of Milwaukee they couldn't care less.

MR. TERHORST: I only heard one comment. I happened to be in New York yesterday and a cabbie voluntarily out of the blue said, "What do you think of the President going to the airport to meet the Redskins?" Now this is a New York cabbie so he was probably a Jet's fan. I said, "I don't know, I thought it was kind of interesting—not many Presidents go out to meet football teams," dancing around the thing to see what he's going to come back with. And he said, "I thought it was terrible. After all he's President of the United States. He shouldn't be out there. He must have better things to do than to go out and meet football teams." A lot of people, I suppose, in Washington thought it was just great that he went out and greeted the Redskins.

QUESTION: We're talking around the subject that I think may be pretty important, but let me ask a question. How did each of these Presidents view the impact of the press corps on public opinion? We seem to have come to that point in talking about the public and the press and the President. Is it something that they even thought about?

Did they in each case view the press as terribly important in shaping public opinion?

MR. REEDY: The answer for my President is yes, he thought it was terribly important. In fact he overestimated the importance of it to a degree that was absolutely astounding, I think.

MR. TERHORST: I would say yes, very much so. I think Jerry Ford looked on the press as the major avenue for reaching the public.

QUESTION: And the attitude of the press would be important in shaping public attitude for him.?

MR. TERHORST: He was very interested in keeping a friendly press corps. And in appearing to be accommodating to what he felt were legitimate things. I think you sense that a little bit even with Reagan today. You know so many times even when just walking to the car he seemingly cannot resist the temptation to answer Sam Donaldson's "Mr. President, what do you think of this?" and he has to say something—either hold his hand up or give him a quip and some of them are pretty good and some of them aren't. But he seems to really feel that he needs to do that.

MR. POWELL: They've got that much better in hand. They taught him this little thing where you shrug and look at your watch and point at Nancy who's already on the helicopter. You're not saying anything but it looks like "Gee whiz, I'd like to stop and talk to you fine people. Duty calls."

MR. REEDY: I think you've got to build in one factor here. One of Johnson's problems was that he was accustomed to the Texas press. What you had in Texas were newspapers that were so intimately entertwined in the power structure in Texas that most of the time what the press was for was what would happen. I think he thought the press caused it to happen. I don't, myself. I think that what was happening was that it was a time in Texas history when most of the owners of newspapers played a very direct role in editorial policy. They were on the same side as most of the dominant economic and political forces in Texas. That means they were on the same side as the people who made things happen. Therefore, when something happened he thought the press was the cause, not realizing that it was just a part of the cause. It never occurred to him that he had managed to buck the Texas press fairly well, because in most of his campaigns the majority of the Texas press was against him.

QUESTION: What about President Carter's attitude?

MR. POWELL: He understood the importance, but he had almost a fatalistic attitude about them in that there wasn't a whole lot you could do with them. You had to do the best you could and bear the burden with as much courage and fortitude as you could muster. He took very little interest, at least insofar as he ever expressed it to me, in the day-to-day operations of dealing with the press, even to the point of what you said at briefings except on very singular occasions or the whole thing we've been talking about, how you go about selling or presenting the White House side of things. An exception was his inclination to talk to them, which he enjoyed, and I think deep down inside he kept thinking if he could just talk to enough of them long enough they would finally understand. I don't know if he's come to the conclusion that that won't help either yet or not.

MR. THOMPSON: Did President Carter consciously during the hostage crisis have Tom Reston and Hodding Carter speak to the press often? We had Tom Reston here a few years ago and he said that he felt that the triumphs, in foreign policy anyway, were always reported by the State Department.

MR. POWELL: Well, it made Hodding a national hero. I tell you the key to that is very technical and very mechanical. At the beginning of the administration, Hodding decided, I have to say without asking me about it—on the other hand if he'd asked me then I probably would have agreed—to allow filming of the State Department's briefings. And of course it comes up with every news press secretary—are you going to allow television cameras in the White House briefings?—which I think would be an absolute disaster. And I said no, it was for the White House. What happened, if you went back to look at it, and it's an exception to what I said earlier about the desire to make everything a White House story, is that if you have two spokesmen saying about the same thing and one of them is saying it before cameras and the other one is not, then networks are going to use what they have a picture of. So the reason you saw so much of the State Department, which suited me all right I must say, was primarily because those briefings were available to camera and mine weren't.

MR. REEDY: One of the interesting things about Lyndon Johnson, was not so much his estimate of the influence of the press but his overestimation of how much influence other politicians had with the press. He was convinced that Jack Kennedy and Bobby Kennedy had the press under complete control. He'd go to extraordinary lengths. I remember once reading an article by Gore Vidal in *Esquire*. It was one of the nastiest bitterest attacks on Bobby Kennedy that I ever read in my life. It was a real hatchet job, so much so that even I, who was not very fond of Bobby, thought that it was a very unfair article. Johnson was then vice president and he called me that morning and he said, "Who planted it?" And I said, "Well, Mr.

President, I don't think anybody had to plant it. Gore Vidal is a very well known writer; *Esquire* is lucky to get anything he wrote." "No, somebody planted it. Tell me, did Bobby Kennedy plant that?" I lifted my chin up off the desk and said, "Excuse me, Mr. President, I thought you said Bobby Kennedy." He said, "Yes, who else would plant such an outrageous puff piece?" Every single thing he read in the press he interpreted as being put in there by Bobby Kennedy. And he literally believed that Pierre Salinger had elected Jack Kennedy President of the United States. I was there when he told Pierre that and Pierre, who was a very sensible guy, could hardly keep from swallowing his tongue.

QUESTION: What did he think was the source of other politicians' influence on the press?

MR. REEDY: He didn't understand. He thought there was some mysterious art here that he couldn't quite dominate, that he couldn't quite master. I think he believed it had something to do with the Ivy League—that the Kennedys had gone to Harvard, whereas he had only gone to Southwest State Teachers College. Of course, Jack Kennedy was extraordinarily successful with certain of the columnists and with certain of the opinion writers in Washington, primarily because he'd been something of a newspaperman himself and he had some idea of what made reporters tick. But the success had very little to do with Kennedy's overall operation as far as the regular flow of news was concerned. I do think that he wasn't doing any better or any worse than any other President. But I could never convince Johnson of that.

QUESTION: How did it influence his behavior, this false estimation both of what others were doing and the impact of the press?

MR. REEDY: Well, for one thing he tried to crowd everybody else out of the paper. Once he became President he learned he could blanket the newspapers. That was the reason for those horrible Saturday morning press conferences. Oh Lord, they were terrible! The other thing was he was constantly accusing the press of being bought up by the Kennedys and sometimes he'd do it to their faces. I remember one day he had Loye Miller in the office. (This was when he was vice president, and Loye was then working for *Time* magazine which was not very friendly to Johnson, but Loye was just doing a routine job.) Johnson started to tell him that he knew all about these briefings that were going on downtown. I think Loye must have thought that he was off his rocker. He literally believed that Bobby Kennedy was holding daily briefings in the Justice Department, the sole purpose of which was to connect Johnson with Bobby Baker and

Billy Sol Estes. The only reason he was having trouble with Bobby Baker and Billy Sol Estes is that he didn't have enough sense to come out and give the press all the facts which would have put an end to it immediately. It wasn't Bobby Kennedy who was pumping that up. It was his own refusal to talk about it.

QUESTION: In your view did that then have policy consequences for the President? Did it influence his policy strategy?

MR. REEDY: Probably not influence his policy but what it did was to influence his style. I do not think that you can separate a President from his style. The President is not just somebody who is there to make a number of decisions. The President is the leader of the country. I think that what he did was to start doing things which appeared to be irrational, not just to the press—that doesn't matter—but to the country as a whole. Over a period of time, I think that a President is not going to be successful unless the public has an image of him as a leader. That's one of the things that really hurt Nixon; he stopped looking like a leader. I think that hurts badly.

QUESTION: Have any of you or all of you ever felt that your first duty was to see, for instance, after Camp David or during Camp David that the full credit for a great achievement would be clearly identified with the President rather than too much be said about Cy Vance's drafting work or some of the other reports that slipped out, or isn't that a pressure? In the private sector very often it is. P.R. people are told, in foundations for instance, you write about the president, and take it easy with other people who may stick their head up too high. The pressure is on, frequently, in the private sector in this regard.

MR. POWELL: I never really thought that was much of a problem; that kind. To the extent credit is given for successes, it tends to be the President's. We really didn't have, but I suppose you could have in an administration a very ambitious Cabinet officer who could create a bit of a problem in that regard. I never really ran into it and don't ever remember worrying two seconds about how did I make sure the President gets credit. It was the other side of it, going toward a problem, of trying to avoid having the President get blamed for every thing that went wrong in the entire federal government.

MR. REEDY: I think sometimes a President deliberately props up a Cabinet officer. He realizes when the policy starts to go bad that public wrath may be deflected. I sometimes wonder if that isn't Mr. Watt's genuine role in the current administration.

MR. TERHORST: Looking at this question both as a reporter and as a press secretary, I have a feeling that they all, including the present occupant of the White House, want to have an opportunity to decide if they personally will make all of the good news that's likely to be made or the important news. I can't think of a President who out of the goodness of his heart said, "Well, I know that's probably the biggest thing coming down the track in my presidency this year, but I'm going to let the secretary of HUD make this announcement or even State or Defense." And partly it's because the Cabinet people are creatures of the President, so he does have a right to make those major announcements if he thinks it will help him politically or help him with Congress because it's his duty as President to make those decisions. In the long run he has to sign off on whatever is done. And there is a tendency, I think, if the news is less favorable, actually in some cases to tell a Cabinet member that it's your job to make that announcement. You can see it right now; look at the game Reagan is playing on economic indicators. If they're good, you know who is going to make those announcements—they are going to come out of the White House press office or out of the President's mouth, if he's available in public to be quoted. And if they're bad then they're made by the Labor Department or the Bureau of Labor Statistics or by the economic advisor or somebody else. I think that's just a normal human reaction.

MR. POWELL: It's legitimate. Cabinet officers don't run for anything. They don't hold their jobs except through the President and they won't have them if he's not elected.

MR. REEDY: I think you must also realize that sometimes Presidents will use this sort of thing as a sort of a litmus test. For example, I am convinced that Kissinger became so very, very prominent in the recognition of China because Nixon was uncertain as to the reaction that he would get. You notice in the early days, Mr. Kissinger was the only name you really saw in the press in connection with all the openings to China. And once it became apparent that the reaction was rather good then all of a sudden the picture became one of Nixon drinking toasts with all the top Chinese officials.

MR. TERHORST: And Kissinger, to his credit, was smart enough to realize that no matter how he and Chou En Lai got along, he needed Nixon's sanctification of the process to make it really sell, both within China and within the U.S.

MR. REEDY: You see a President really doesn't have to worry. If something is going well a President can always take charge, crowd whoever did it off the front page. That's no problem.

QUESTION: Well, I was sitting here trying to think of the right paraphrase, listening to all this, and some of you are going to have to help me out on this because I'm not sure exactly how to phrase it. Is it better for our government to have a good press secretary and not much of a President or a bad press secretary and a good President?

MR. REEDY: You're speaking of an oxymoron.

QUESTION: I'm groping for the right way to say that.

MR. TERHORST: I don't think it's possible. I really don't. If you've got a good President you've got a good press secretary. The best press secretary in the White House, I always thought, was the President. If he was on target and he was saying things that sounded newsy and important, I don't care if they were plus or minus, necessarily, but if they're newsy and important it made my job a lot easier and I think that when Jody was there or George, if the President had something worth saying that was newsy everybody looked good. And if the news is bad and dismal, none of us looked too good. I just think the two go hand in hand. I don't think you can separate the two. I don't know how you can have a President of disrepute, as it were, and have a popular press secretary. The only one I can really think of is Richard Nixon, and to a degree, I suppose, Johnson in some of the throes of the Vietnam anguish and agony. The press office then didn't look too bright either.

MR. REEDY: Actually he kept most of Vietnam away from the press office, shuttled it over to Defense. Now to a certain extent though it reminds me of one of Helen Thomas's pet sayings, that is that the press office should be primarily responsible to the press. You know, she asks a question that's self-answering. Who pays your salary? Well, anybody who doesn't know who pays the salary isn't bright enough to walk into the office.

QUESTION: I'm groping now for something, I think it was at the end of your book, Jerry, and it would be nice of you to state it for us and see what we think of it. Each press secretary has got to serve two or three constituencies, the President, press and the public. How do you rate those responsibilities?

MR. TERHORST: Yes, that's true. That's the way I tried to look at my job. They are present and they are not of equal priority. Obviously you do work for the President in that you hold your own job by virtue of his having chosen you and, if he doesn't want you there, out you go sooner or later. It's impossible for a press secretary to tell a President, "No, I'm not leaving. I'm sticking around." So to that extent you are a creature of the presidency. And so your job is to serve the President.

George quoted, I think, "Your job is to convey what the President wants said to the public." That's obviously a major priority. On the other hand, I did feel it was my duty to help the press grasp as best I could, knowing they couldn't sit in every meeting or be party or privy to every conversation that made up a decision we were talking about, to try to help them understand some of the color of the event, some of the internals of the event and in that respect be an advocate for the press. I'm sure we all did this. Jody did it and George, too, going to a staffer and saying, "Well, I've got to have more than that, that's fine—but who was at the table, where did they sit?" You get these questions. And as George said, they're terribly stylistic. The press sometimes wants to know who sat at a meeting on the right or the left or across the table, what they were wearing. Presumably that's nice for features, but they really do want to know who sat where and who was doing what to whom at the moment. Most of it never gets in the paper but I think it helps color their understanding or helps shape their understanding of what transpired. But in terms of the public aspect of it, I felt that if I couldn't do a pretty good job of explaining to the press what the President was trying to do or had just done, the public would not understand it at all. If I couldn't get it through the press, if I couldn't make the press see this as a rational, necessary, logical decision that had been made in view of the events, there's no way that the public would get the message. I hope that was what you were driving at.

MR. POWELL: I'd like to make another distinction here. You've got to remember something and that is the President is the United States. Jerry's absolutely right. It's one thing to try to give the press a feel for what is actually happening. But suppose the press secretary differed with the President on policy. What would happen to the United States if the President stated one thing and his official spokesman stated something else? This isn't even a question of sycophancy. It's just that we have a Constitution that says all executive powers shall be vested in the President. Not like Congress.

I always looked at it, without a great deal of mental turmoil, that you work for the President and as long as you can do that in good conscience and consistent with the same standards and ethical considerations you apply to anything else that you did, you do it. If at some point you can't do that, then you don't do it. And considerations of basic kindness and humanity—if a reporter wants something and you can do it and it will make his life easier and he's a half-way decent person you do it, if it does not conflict with that other responsibility which is to speak for the President. Speaking for the President, as George has said, is the nuts and bolts of the thing. There are a lot of other things that have to be done, but that is the guts of the responsibility. There may be some people that congenitally are not suited to speak for someone else, and they may be much better people for that. But if you can't speak for the President, then you ought not to be doing it. If you're constantly caught up in all sorts of mental and moral dilemmas about whether you can go out and defend something that you disagree with then, as my boss used to say on occasion, run for office yourself.

MR. REEDY: It is not a parliamentary government, we do not have cabinet government.

QUESTION: Are there any cases where you're either called on or moved to try and have some policy influence? Jerry, for example, in that terribly important case, in your relationship with President Ford, did you seek to have some influence on that decision because it was so vital to your own position?

MR. TERHORST: No. Unfortunately, in my case, that decision was made before I heard about it. In fact I just heard about it the evening before and the President wanted to announce it the next morning. In fact, everything was being arranged—even with time to get an answer out of San Clemente, where Nixon was, the following morning. It was a case of do it at that moment. So I had no input at all on the policy decision. In fact very few people had any input. It really stemmed from, as President Ford said in his book and as we said at the time, the fact that he had decided one morning over Labor Day 1974 to ask his legal counsel and long-time friend from Michigan, Phil Buchen, what were the constititutional problems with issuing a pardon—and keep it to yourself, Phil, just tell me about it. As he says, it took about three days to really go into it with great detail, checking case histories and everything else, everything that had been written in judicial literature and history about the nature of the pardon power. And it was only after that that he talked to a couple of people to find out if Nixon was interested in it, what would be the ramifications in terms of the special prosecutor's claim on the Watergate documents. Obviously he wanted to make sure Leon Jaworski was not going to sound off critically about it if he had done it, so Jaworski had to be included; Buchen had a talk with Jaworski privately. But when I heard about the decision, it was all done. It would have been futile to object. It would have amounted to kicking the floor, or something.

QUESTION: Well, are there occasions when you seek to influence decisions? Or is it essentially a policy neutral type of job?

MR. TERHORST: No, no.

MR. REEDY: It's up to the President.

MR. TERHORST: It depends. If he asks you, you have a right, if you really feel that you've really got to say something, to say it. But there's no reason why he has to take your advice. I suppose half the time they don't.

MR. REEDY: I think you can learn more about the White House by studying the court of Louis XIV than you will by sending in people to send out questionnaires and ask how the decisions were made. An awful lot of presidential decisionmaking reminds me of the old gag about the businessman who had to hire a new secretary. They gave him three choices. His assistant said about one girl, "She's not very good at stenography but she speaks excellent Spanish and we're opening up a Spanish office. The second girl is very good at filing, and the third girl is very good at this, that, and the other." The business- man replied, "I'll take the one with the size forty bust." Don't look for too much of an overly stylized way of making decisions. They're overly stylized if the President wants them that way. If he doesn't want them that way they aren't.

MR. POWELL: They are more that way in retrospect just because of the intellectual need to try to impose some order. So you tend to go back—even when you're looking at your own behavior there is a tendency to impose a great deal more logic and order on the thing than was ever present.

MR. REEDY: You see the order later on because obviously there is some form or order to it. God made the universe and there's order in the universe. That doesn't mean you understand it at the time it's going on or that you can predict it.

QUESTION: How much does a President seek out in advance your advice—I'm thinking particularly in President Carter's case on the malaise speech—on what he's going to say. After all you're supposed to be the guy that's the expert on what impact it's going to have on the public. You're not a speechwriter but do you get the drafts well in advance and then comment on them?

MR. POWELL: I did on all the important ones and more of the ones of lesser importance than I wanted, as a matter of fact. But again I think that varies with the President. It's not always a question of seeking, either. It depends on how that process works. If you're there at an early point, as Jerry was saying to the contrary a while ago, when something is being considered then you have your chance if you have something to say, even if it's as mundane such as "Well, if you want to do it, do that, but I suggest you don't do it that particular way because that will never fly." I think anybody that has good access to a President also has a great deal of responsibility about how they use that access. I always felt a great deal of constraint, even if and when the President asked, about what type of advice I gave. I tried not to let the fact that I could see him more frequently, perhaps, than someone who had a great deal more expertise in a particular area give my point of view an inordinate weight with him because I didn't think that was fair to him or to the other person on the staff or in the interest of good public policy. I can't describe how you draw that line between the general sort of discussion of an issue, which I felt was legitimate and was at the generalist level that I felt confident to deal with, and when you are spilling over into an area that you really are not competent to argue and you ought to be careful about abusing your access.

MR. THOMPSON: After our full day session of the senior White House reporters, we came away with the impression that this was indeed a very rough, tough, no holds barred game, that so far as inducements, incentives, alluring attractions were concerned that your particular Presidents and Presidents in general had hesitated at nothing—they'd offer money, they'd offer women, they'd offer fame and fortune to reporters who would do or not do certain things.

We also came away with the impression that these several senior White House reporters felt they were like herded animals. Helen Thomas, for instance, told about Reagan's trip six months ago or so to Baltimore where at six in the morning they were herded into helicopters and flown over to the poor family that Reagan wanted to visit and appear with him on television, and that life for reporters was not much different than Hobbes's nasty, poor, brutish, and short. Dawn to dusk, indignities, pressure.

MR. TERHORST: God, I feel sorry for Helen. I wonder why she keeps doing it, day after day after day. I wonder what the reward is for going through this hell?

QUESTION: To say "Thank you, Mr. President."

MR. TERHORST: To get to be invited to Charlottesville perhaps.

MR. THOMPSON: Is all of this a myth or an illusion in the minds of these reporters or do things of this kind go on?

MR. POWELL: Life is certainly tough all over. They don't have a particularly easy job by any means. Most press offices that have any sense at all go out of their way to try to hold that sort of stuff to a minimum. If there is any trend over the last ten years or so it is that every administration tries to figure out what else they can do in terms of care and feeding and pampering. I don't mean that it can't be a tough, frustrating, tiring sort of job with the press. I think Nixon probably was the first to seize on that and it probably benefited him some. Since then I think the rest of us have sort of tried to think of one more way to drink with someone or to have more time to do this, that, or the other, or take their wives and children on a foreign trip. I don't think it's bought any administration one damn thing.

MR. TERHORST: I don't know what the threats and promises might have been. The senior White House reporters who have told you this—I wonder why they are not writing it. There's a hell of a news story in it if true.

MR. REEDY: They write it occasionally.

MR. TERHORST: Threats and promises from the White House?

MR. POWELL: Such as?

MR. REEDY: I never heard of the women thing.

MR. POWELL: Money?

MR. REEDY: No, not money either. One of the biggest stories of the Johnson administration was when he'd get those people in and say, "Look, I'm going to make big men out of you."

MR. TERHORST: Oh, yes.

MR. REEDY: I think a better way of saying it is that the story they're giving you is rather accurate all right but it's way out of balance. Of course Presidents try to control the press. Good God, who doesn't try to control the press? Every businessman tries to control the press, every union leader tries to control the press, every college president tries to control the press, everybody tries to control the press. The President has a few more weapons in his hand but in my judgment, he's the man that gets the least out of controlling the press. I don't think it does him the slightest bit of good. You can control individual reporters and you have some who are members either of the world's oldest or second oldest profession—that is not unknown. You have others who have a very high degree of integrity. Yes, there are threats. Johnson was always threatening to cut this person off, cut that person off. He would give some people exclusive photographs. There may have been some parts of the country down in Texas where a little bit of money was passed under the counter. That I don't know. I don't think you can do it in Washington, D.C. And as far as the women are concerned, any reporter in Washington that can't get women doesn't deserve to have the job. There are certain things that just go with it. There's alleged glamour to it.

But what is really happening here is that there is a constant struggle going on between the press and the President. The struggle is due to the fact that they see different worlds. The President is a politician, the journalists are journalists. They both have their strengths, they both have their weaknesses. And what you are getting here is the side of the journalist. Now, if you were to call in Presidents and ask them, what you'd get is a horrible story of the abuse they take, of the complete irresponsibility of the press. The funny part is both sides are right, you know.

MR. POWELL: And the manipulation, the attempts to manipulate are both ways. Every press secretary has, by the giving and withholding of information, attempted to influence coverage, where the story runs, who gets it first, how you're treated over the other reporters. Every time you pick up a phone or engage in an attempt through rewards and punishments, more often implicit than explicit as they usually are, it enables you to help them, to talk to them, to deal with them on that story. The most famous old line "Ah, you'll come out a lot better if you talk to me than if you don't. If you don't get somebody back to me by four o'clock I'm just going to have to go ahead and write it."

MR. REEDY: This is a pluralistic society in which we live. We have a pluralistic form of government and what that means is that there's a lot of tugging and hauling. There's an adversarial form of government, an adversarial form of relationships, and anytime you listen to one side of it you're going to get a horror story.

QUESTION: But you wouldn't have it otherwise?

MR. REEDY: No, I sure would not. I'm perfectly willing to pat the press on the head, bandage up some of the bad wounds if it will help any. I'm perfectly willing to pat Presidents on the head and bandage up their wounds. But believe it or not, society is not threatened by it. And it's not as bad as it used to be. You ought to read what some of the newspapers said about Abraham Lincoln during the Civil War. He was once described as a big black baboon. Everybody's very fond of quoting Thomas Jefferson about how if he had his choice between a government without newspapers and newspapers without government he'd take the newspapers without government. That was before he became President. You ought to see what he wrote after he became President. This is old. It's been going on since there have been newspapers and I just can't get excited about it.

MR. TERHORST: I don't know of any threats, so-called. I suppose somebody might say, well, the way you act we're not going to give you any stories any more, because I just can't trust you after what you did. Perhaps that's a threat.

QUESTION: One of the reporters who was here at this session, speaking of a recent administration, said that a high staffer in the White House in that administration had, in talking to him, showed him a picture of his family and said, "You've got an awfully nice looking wife and children." And the reporter took this as a threat.

MR. TERHORST: If he didn't write that he was not a good journalist. Boy, if that had happened to me I would have written that in a hurry! I tell you I could have made a lot of news out of that and have a field day with it. Probably earn myself not only brownie points with my paper and my colleagues but probably gotten some better treatment out of the White House if I wasn't getting good treatment!

MR. POWELL: Well, you couldn't have written it unless you had at least asked a question after that. It's kind of hard to make a story out of and you can see why he did it orally rather than in print. This guy showed me a picture of my wife and family and we all know what *that* means.

MR. TERHORST: Just to give you a small insight into this: when I first came to Washington I spent a couple of years, as most reporters do, covering the Congress. In 1960 when Kennedy became President, I was assigned, through a series of events, to the White House and also became bureau chief. You would be surprised how many people on the White House staff suddenly discovered my existence. My wife and I had more nice invitations to various things, including state dinners at the White House starting with that time. This was topped only when I became press secretary. Then I became very important to journalists I used to admire in awe all the way from New York to California. Important publishers suddenly discovered that I was the press secretary to the White House. I'm sure the the same thing happened to Jody and to George. So this business of promising or purporting to promise or currying favor or whatever you're trying to call it, really does work two ways. It's just human nature. It's just the way people exist. Somebody becomes the head of a department here at UVA, and I'm sure suddenly he gets a lot more attention than he did before from people who find it important to know him better. Or vice versa, to have them know him better.

MR. POWELL: And frankly when you get into that game, and this is a little bit at an angle from what we're dealing with, there are all sorts of people in institutions and interests in Washington that have much more in the way of resources to play at than the White House does. The White House is really at somewhat of a disadvantage in many ways. Yes, you've got three or four slots for reporters at a state dinner and so you get them in there and then you can do some stuff with the Kennedy Center and you've got a few of those to hand out and there are other sorts of social things that you can provide. But unless you happen to be independently wealthy you can't compete with your own personal resources with the sort of entertaining and wining and dining and that sort of thing at the White House that a middle level interest group in Washington can do, for example.

MR. TERHORST: They all have expense accounts.

MR. POWELL: Yes. Or the other sort of favors, whether it's football tickets or you name it. There are probably six dozen operations in Washington that can do more of that for journalists and get more from it than the White House can.

MR. REEDY: The one thing the President does have, however, and it's a very potent weapon, is access to the press.

MR. TERHORST: The ultimate reward is if you can arrange a one-on-one interview.

MR. REEDY: The difficulty with it, however, in my experience is that the things that the President can get out sometimes aren't worth having. I remember on one occasion where a certain journalist, he's now dead but I'm not going to name him anyway, went way out of his way to cultivate Johnson—even had his kids dress up in cute cowboy costumes. He managed to wrangle a lunch one day where he said at the top of his voice, "The trouble with the press is they're a bunch of cry babies." So naturally he started getting all kinds of exclusive pictures, not from me I can assure you. But the interesting thing about it, I never saw one single thing that did Johnson any good that he got out of it. Not one thing. You can control certain features of the press, certain aspects of it. That can be done. But when the President sends troops into Vietnam and a bunch of people get killed, you can't call in any due bills from the press and have them write nice stories about how those kids weren't killed. That is the difficulty with the President. What a President does speaks so much louder than anything he can say that many of the fancy Dan press relations which do serve other institutions at other levels don't serve him.

MR. POWELL: The events tend to overpower those.

MR. REEDY: The President is the only person who cannot escape history. If a volcano goes off, he's somewhere, he's got to react to it. Some of them react a little too fast. Actually the first place in the world the practice of fancy Dan type of press relationships stops is in the White House because there is no percentage in it.

QUESTION: What is the ongoing attitude of the White House press corps? I mean just on a day-to-day basis. Is it adversarial or do they look at it as a business; they have to deal with you and they're friendly? How does it work on a day-to-day basis?

MR. REEDY: Depends on the day.

MR. POWELL: Yes, it does. If you're in a mess, you're in a mess. But it's not adversarial, I think, with the White House press corps. You and they do have to live almost together. You're right there. You travel together. Except in the worst circumstances, you have to maintain, and both sides have an interest in maintaining, some sort of decent relationship so that you can get along and that people aren't just feeling miserable and uptight the whole time.

MR. REEDY: I think Ron Ziegler was the only one who ever really was at cross purposes. I'm not sure that was Ron's fault.

QUESTION: You raise an interesting question. How did you determine who was going to get in to see the President? People in the press corps are always asking if they can have individual interviews with the President. How would you go about determining that? How much time you can give them and all that stuff?

MR. POWELL: Obviously, to some extent, you can certainly exclude some people. I wasn't going to send Bob Novak in to sit down and chitchat with Carter on frequent occasions. Novak knew that. Carter knew that. I knew that. I don't think Novak ever took that as a threat or anything. It was just a waste of time for me and he would have thought I was stupid if I had done that.

QUESTION: You would have gotten the wrong story out of it.

MR. POWELL: So you obviously don't send somebody in there that you know is carrying a weapon to spend time with the President. And then beyond that, it depends on what you're looking for. You may be looking for a particular story on a particular subject. You may be looking for just general good feelings and you ought to let this guy in. I've even done it, on occasion, when somebody I thought was a decent reporter was having a little trouble back with the paper, or something like that, and I thought it might help him out to get something. I'm sure everybody else has done that too, which I suppose is a hell of a way to use the highest office in the land, but it's probably as good as a lot of others.

MR. REEDY: You've got to start with something. You don't send anybody in to see the President. The President decides whether he's going to see him.

MR. POWELL: Well, that's true.

MR. REEDY: But number two, I think that what you do, the recommendations that you make to the President, you hope the President will follow. You do want to get opinion leaders. Now by opinion leaders I'm talking about the press. There is such a thing as pack journalism. It's even worse for photographers. You watch sometimes when one photographer takes a picture. Every photographer within fifty miles runs up and snaps the same thing real quick. There are certain types of journalists and if they write a story everybody else is going to write that story. So I think that's one of the considerations you take into account. Another consideration that you take into account is that you may feel that somebody in that category has reached a stage of nastiness where the only thing you can possibly do is see if the President himself can't soften the blow; you might do that. And of course the worst part was that Johnson made so many arrangements all by himself without telling anybody, some of which turned out disastrously.

QUESTION: Can you say something more about this matter of leadership within the media? To what extent do they have an impact on each other? But beyond, the TV and the print media interaction and relationships and the impact of TV on the print media and vice versa.

MR. REEDY: You have to realize one thing about the TV media and that is that the sheer clumsiness of the equipment has lot to do with what the TV media actually does. It seems to me one of the greatest mating dances always took place when somebody would come out of the White House—like McNamara after his conference with the President—and the three network reporters would get together and each one would decide which question they were going to ask. The reason was that they got fifty dollars or so extra every time their face appeared on TV. And so they'd divide up the three questions and their cameramen would carefully put the NBC camera on the NBC man when he was asking his question and the others would only record the answers.

But a tremendous amount of news consists of journalists talking to other journalists. And it's not necessarily an illegitimate process. What they are really doing is pooling information and I hope they keep it up. I have no problem with that. You have to realize something else though and that is that a tremendous amount of the news process consists of a symbiotic relationship between the journalist and the people they're covering. They influence each other.

QUESTION: Is there a specific influence present with the development of television? Does that help shape what the print folks are doing or do the print folks really determine what TV's going to cover?

MR. TERHORST: My feeling is that a piece well written and placed in an important journal has much more impact on television than the world generally knows about. For example, you could see that in spades during Watergate. If the *Washington Post* or the *New York Times* ran a story in print in the morning on some new fresh aspect of Watergate, you could predict what the six o'clock or the network news that night would feature: it would be a TV version of that story. Whereas if TV develops a story you cannot guarantee that it will necessarily turn up in, say, the *New York Times* or the

Washington Post. It might get picked up and they might make a reference to it but they won't make their feature piece out of, "NBC said today that. . . ." That's happens once in a while but not nearly to the degree that print journalism influences TV mainly, I suppose, because we have a funny thing in this country and a lot of people don't stop to realize it, but I'm convinced it effects the way journalism and news flows generally. The sun comes up in New York and all the editors for the Associated Press, UPI, and Reuters who are in America covering America, and the three networks get up and they see the morning papers. The *New York Times*—that's their first glimpse of what's going to happen that day. The news flow and the sun travels together across the country. It takes almost more than twenty-four hours for a Los Angeles story to turn up in New York. A New York story or an East Coast story will turn up in Los Angeles within twenty minutes if it's any good. You can't defeat that. That's the way the sun goes.

MR. POWELL: You also have the mechanical and personal sort of things. The *Washington Post* and the *Los Angeles Times* share the same wire service. The *Washington Post* would rather die and burn in hell than use a *Los Angeles Times* story on the front page. They just don't want to do it. The *LA Times* has had, they're doing better now, but they've had a problem for years because of their late date and time each day in getting the paper to print; they can't get it back in time to get enough copies around Washington. It's a good paper, so enough of opinion makers and decisionmakers and other journalists read the thing. So you'll quite often see a scoop of serious proportions in the *Los Angeles Times* or maybe the *Wall Street Journal* pick up on the same story, as though it had appeared for the first time. And if you'd only read that paper you'd never know that this story was written three days ago.

MR. REEDY: There's another factor here you have to watch for which is that because television only treats physical events, you will discover there's quite a divergence between what appears on television and what appears in the press over the evening TV shows. The shows will often give big play to a story and when I pick up the *Milwaukee Journal* the next morning it will be on about page eight back with a couple of truss ads and when I see the *Post* a few days later, the same thing will happen. There is a limitation to what you can do on television. And the limitation is a very interesting one. Before television what you would do would be to take the story to the reporters. Now what you do is take the reporters to the story. You set the story up somewhere. An awful lot of things that happen today, and I think this is one of the major impacts of television, is that things are set up so there will be television coverage. When you plan a presidential parade route, for example, you have a long talk in advance about precisely where you're going to have the stands for the TV cameras. And usually somewhere along the lines you're going to have a one armed veteran of the Spanish American War that will salute as he goes by, or you'll have school kids to wave little flags, such as those cute little Chinese school children in Hawaii. And you can be sure wherever there's a television camera somebody will run out and present the President with a bunch of posies. You get an awful lot of that. Television has a habit, not of shaping the story but of shaping the conditions under which the story will be presented.

QUESTION: Is there such a thing as leadership among the White House press corps or is it everybody reacting to the President?

MR. POWELL: You fairly quickly learn who the two or three usually dominant personalities amongst the White House regulars are. I use that term advisedly—"dominant personalities." It may or may not have to do so much with what they write or what they put on the air. It's seldom that you get a bad reporter, one that doesn't do the work at least reasonably well that can occupy that role. But they don't have to be the best reporter, in fact I've found some of the best reporters don't ever occupy that part.

MR. REEDY: Or not necessarily the most prestigious paper either.

MR. POWELL: That's right. It doesn't relate to a lot of the other things we've been talking about here. But there are people that talk a lot or that talk loud, and they're just the sort of people that in any sort of small group situation would tend to dominate, to impose their opinions and be leaders. Every White House press corps has them.

QUESTION: Can you give us some examples, Jody?

MR. POWELL: Helen [Thomas] is one, Jack Nelson, no not now because Jack doesn't fit as a regular—I'm talking about the White House regulars, people that are at the White House eight and ten hours a day now, which Nelson is not. And outside of that you've got circles and groups of reporters and journalists that operate in their own little circle. The crowd at The Class, which I still frequent on occasion in much more relaxed circumstances, is an example of that. Jack Nelson is a dominant member of a crowd of journalists that do most of their after-hours drinking in a bar called The Class Reunion. That is a group and they talk to one another there. Most of them are not White House regulars.

MR. REEDY: When I was there the dominant personalities were Chuck Bailey of the *Minneapolis Tribune*, certainly not a most prestigious paper. Also Doug Kiker with the *New York Herald Tribune* and Bill Lawrence of ABC who is now dead. But they were not the most important reporters. I'd say the more important ones were people like John Pomfret of the *New York Times* and Merriman Smith and quite possibly Frank Cormier. But nevertheless, those three men were constantly talking, they were having an impact, that impact that Jody Powell's describing.

QUESTION: They were leaders in the sense that they were sort of cue givers for others?

MR. TERHORST: Every group looked up to them in some way. Bill Lawrence gained his fame not on ABC but, as you know, in the *New York Times*. That's why ABC hired him because he was so good.

MR. REEDY: Sam Donaldson is another one.

MR. TERHORST: Pete Lisagor used to be another.

MR. POWELL: Charlie Mohr when he was at the *Times*. And that's a case of a person who does not have a particularly outgoing or dominant personality, but his influence was because of his being so good and so precise and just a top-notch reporter.

MR. REEDY: I remember the day Doug Kiker walked into the lobby and shouted at the top of his voice, "Welcome to credibility gap." Now, actually he picked the phrase out of a speech that was made by Secretary of Labor Goldberg, a man who had been chief counsel to the AFL-CIO. He had made a speech saying that we had to be careful of the credibility gap. But I think what put it into the minds of the press was just Doug Kiker walking into the lobby that day and saying, "Welcome to credibility gap."

MR. POWELL: That can happen. Donaldson is a master of that, just setting the tone, getting people headed in a particular direction. Sometimes it's more of a feel or an attitude.

MR. TERHORST: More atmospheric, sometimes, than story-oriented.

MR. POWELL: I remember about three or four days before the Camp David summit, we were somewhere out in the Rocky Mountain west, I think, and the President was fixing to get on the airplane and Donaldson shouted out some question about sending American troops to the Middle East as part of any agreement that might come out of this summit that was going to take place in four days. And the President gave some sort of brush-off answer. Donaldson turned around and said, "My God, they're going to send American troops." And they raced off. It took us about three days to get that thing quieted down. Everybody got on it. We went back and looked at what the President said. It was something like "I don't have any inclination to do that or it was short of "Never under any circumstances would I agree to this, no matter what Begin and Sadat say would I ever send one American soldier to the Middle East, ever as long as I live." And there the thing stood.

QUESTION: How do you explain the Barbara Walters phenomenon? She was created by Presidents. Not terribly bright but always sitting by the fireplace, and gets to every President.

MR. TERHORST: It didn't hurt for her to be a woman in that environment at that moment in time. I don't mean that in a sex-oriented way. I'm thinking of the fact that at that time when Barbara was coming on the scene, there weren't really very many good female journalists covering Presidents. There really weren't. Helen Thomas was almost an exception. But very few. It was overwhelmingly a male press corps, on the networks as well as on the press.

MR. REEDY: That was part of it. I think that Barbara Walters has somewhat the same influence that Spanish bullfighters have to see how close they can get to the horns of that bull. There's obviously danger in it, when she's interviewing. And I think there's a little sort of a psychological gamesmanship.

MR. TERHORST: The master of that is our Italian friend, Fallaci. She's terrific.

MR. POWELL: Let me say this about Barbara. Barbara does work at it; she works at it and she touches all the bases. When she sets out to get the President for an interview for her special or her this or that or the other, I guarantee you she does not miss a lick. You'll come home at nine-thirty at night and your daughter will say to you, "Are you going to give Barbara Walters that interview?" Almost literally, she goes at it with all four feet. And I don't say that in an uncomplimentary way at all.

MR. REEDY: I'm wondering whether there may not be a certain trace of suicidal complex involved in Presidents. Jack Kennedy was always recognizing Sarah McClendon. Before going into a press conference Jack would say, "I'm not going to recognize Sarah McClendon," yet by God, he would. I have all respect for that woman but everybody thinks she's sort of scatterbrained. Yet she comes up with some questions, she'll penetrate. Again, I think it was like bull fighting.

QUESTION: How about Mary McGory, is she another type?

QUESTION: Certainly she is.

QUESTION: Does she ask questions at press conferences?

MR. POWELL: Yes, but that's the only time she ever shows up at the White House.

MR. TERHORST: Mary is really an essayist.

QUESTION: Would you say something about television, about the extent to which you are able to control the conditions under which news is going to be made or exhibited on television? I recall a friend of mine who helped the speaker of the House from time to time with press relations. What he says is, it would be nice if you could get TV in particular to come to your setting, which is the speaker's office, rather than having you go to their setting because when they set it up that's quite a different situation. You have the office and that kind of thing when you're at home. It raises a question about how much you feel the press secretary is really in a position to control that on the TV side. I suppose with the White House you're in a lot better position than most other politicians. But could you say something about just how you experiment with different settings for the press conference?

MR. REEDY: Well, you see the point is that they can't set the cameras up unless you give them a place to set them up; it's that simple.

MR. POWELL: You can pretty well control that but again the question is how much it gets you. Television skill has been learned so long that there are not a whole lot of refinements you can make to it. Everybody says, OK, you can get it set up so that the guy looks to his best advantage. You try to avoid situations that look silly or stupid and sometimes you mess up. But I don't know that it gets you a lot. On the day-to-day sort of stuff, when they're just standing out there in front of the north front, that sticks. They're going to be there and say what they please. That's where the damage is done.

MR. REEDY: Rose garden rubbish.

MR. TERHORST: If you have a briefing that is likely to do the President some good, or the President feels he's going to look good as a result of it, you can tilt the process a little bit by arranging that briefing in a suitable setting early enough in the day to make sure that the networks can get their video tape cans to their editors in New York in time for the show. You can't guarantee they'll use it but at least you've got a shot at the show. And if you have bad news or a lousy report, hold it off and do it at a time when it's impossible to be on the evening news.

MR. POWELL: Or just deal with it with a briefing where there are no cameras, which won't necessarily keep it off the air because they can still walk out there and do it. Last night you had Martin Feldstein; they wanted to get something on the air about things looking up and the President was right and the economy is getting better. If they had had almost anybody come in and say that at a regular briefing, you'd have never made it. But they made the thing available to cameras, they gave them somebody high up enough in the administration that it had some clout to it. It also was a good choice because he established credibility early by differing with some things with stories coming out that he didn't think things were as rosy as some of his supplysiders did. They made a good choice. I think a better one than Reagan for example, even though he's higher in the official hierarchy. And they got a decent play for it.

MR. REEDY: You've got to realize one thing and that is that timing may be the most important form of control there is. For many years the White House has been embarrassed by congressional insistence on passing the Captive Nations resolution. Congress does it every year and the White House and State Department wish they would all jump in the nearest toilet and pull the chain. But it's very simple. The President must issue the proclamation but he does it at four or five o'clock Saturday afternoon. And believe me you would practically have to announce the second coming of Christ at five o'clock on a Saturday afternoon to get it on a network show or even get it in the newspapers. You can do things like that. Of course if the story is really important it's no help to you because they'll start picking it up Monday, but on a story like Captive Nations you can have some control.

MR. TERHORST: I think that is endemic because now, you know, that I work for Ford Motor Company and I'm in public relations pure and simple, you can bet your life that when we have a quarterly report that doesn't show any earnings, I'm not going to feed that to the Washington press at prime time. I'm going to give that to them as late as I can on a busy news day and hope it just falls in the crack. Whereas if it's a good one, you can bet your life I'll try to arrange it; I might even try to get Irving R. Levine or somebody to comment on it and give them an interview with somebody and play it up. That part of the thing, as George says, is a matter of timing. You do have some control over when you drop news at the White House.

MR. REEDY: Let me also add that I think technology in the next few years is going to make a very fast change in this. We've had more and more miniaturization of the television cameras and it is now possible to have a camera that's not much larger than you can fit in the palm of your hand. It's too expensive at the moment and there are all kinds of other problems. But they'll be solved. You're going to reach a point where in terms of access the TV networks are going to be in about the same position as the old fashioned writing reporter; all he needed was a pencil and paper and he could borrow those if he forgot to bring them with him when he went down to work in the morning. Now that doesn't mean they're going to do the same thing because you still have the limitations that are inherent in the electronic media. And there's only certain things you can do with the electronic media. But at the moment, as long as the equipment is still as clumsy as it is, you do have this problem. The cameras must be set up and you do have more control.

MR. POWELL: They're going to have a lot more stuff soon. When they went from film to videotape, it made a tremendous difference, in the sense that it expanded their news day. They could get stuff on the air. Now they can actually feed it in live if they need to. Before, with anything past mid-afternoon you were safe from the nets because they could never turn it around in time to get it out.

QUESTION: Do press secretaries make an effort to reach the première columnists who at a given point in time have an influence on intellectual elites, the Restons and earlier the Lippmanns? I suppose Johnson, no matter what he had done by the time he had his full term, couldn't have done much with Lippmann.

MR. REEDY: Actually he could do better with Lippmann than he could with most of the others. Johnson blew it with the intellectuals. They were fascinated by him; they were like moths flickering around the candle; it was raw power. He had an irresistible attraction for the kind of men that had spent most of their lives in an ivory tower. And if he had had any sense he could have had them eating out of his hand. But he didn't. The man who was a real specialist at that was Jack Kennedy. He understood how to do it. I'll never forget that campaign he ran at Harvard. One of my friends is a professor of law at Harvard and once he described it to me. It was orchestrated down to the finest point. But as far as the average press secretary is concerned, I don't think he would have a chance. I don't know about the rest of them, but generally speaking I had too much to do.

MR. POWELL: Yes, that was the problem. I really wish I had paid more attention to those jokers in a way but they like to do business over leisurely lunches where you go out and sit down and you have a drink and a nice bottle of wine and a nice meal and then it's two-thirty in the afternoon and you've dealt with a number of things in a vaguely intellectual fashion, more vague than intellectual. Then you hope that from this flows something or other. I mean there are differences. There are those with whom you can do straight business over the telephone. OK, I've got something for you, you've got something for me. But it's hard to do that and do the press secretary's job because you don't have time.

MR. REEDY: I did a lot more of that when I was executive director of the Senate Democratic policy. I'd have lunch with Stewart Alsop a couple of times a week, another with Roscoe Drummond or somebody who was in town. I was never able to do that when I became press secretary. For the press secretary there's a lot of nit-picking details. Just a little question of eighty-five hotel reservations or having to call American Airlines and say, "I want a 707 laid down at Andrews field in twenty minutes." That does occupy a lot of your time.

MR. TERHORST: I think the biggest shock I had in going to the White House as press secretary was discovering that I was not only the press secretary and spokesman for the President but perhaps more importantly on a day-to-day, hourly basis I was administrator and boss of a fairly large shop of people who got sick or weren't there. Work had to be juggled and things had to be done and some were incompetent and some got tearful and some didn't show up. You're constantly managing the shop as well being an administrator of a fairly large group of people.

MR. POWELL: You're talking about thirty, forty, fifty people.

MR. TERHORST: As well as trying to do the prime job.

MR. POWELL: And they mirror the problems of any other group of employees. They've got problems with their husband or problems with their wife or their mamma died and they need to go home or they're starting to drink a little too much. Or they get themselves in financial trouble and you are stupid enough to co-sign a note. I've got one I'm still watching with some concern.

MR. REEDY: You also have a lot of liaison work. I know one of the things that saved me the most was very carefully setting up a relationship with the secret service. They saved my neck sometimes. They could always get hints as to where the President was going. Johnson dearly loved to keep me and everybody else around the place in the dark as to when he was going to go somewhere. He claimed it was to keep his options open. And he thought the only reason the press wanted to know is so they could write stories that Johnson was going to Texas. That's not what they wanted to know. What they wanted to know was whether they could schedule a dinner for that weekend with their families.

MR. POWELL: Plus, there are no two groups on the face of this earth that despise each other more than secret service agents and reporters. The press office is always in the middle. They just don't like one another. They're totally different breeds of people. And it's the secret service that's keeping them inside the ropes and pushing the cameramen around. They scream and shout at one another and sometimes they even trade blows. The press office is always in the middle. The other reason you need a good relationship with the secret service is that you need to be able to say, "Look, how about helping me out on this one and ease off on these guys over here and can we let the cameras move a little bit here, there?" And you can't, no matter what your authority is. You may think you've got the authority to tell them what to do. Their response is they will do it that one time.

MR. REEDY: You can always get formal compliance.

MR. POWELL: Yes, that's right, but the next time you're really into it. So you have to deal with those guys on a very personal basis, get to know them, understand their problems.

MR. REEDY: I think I was pretty lucky in that Rufus Youngblood was a very good guy to work with; he was head of White House detail when I was there. I was luckier than other press secretaries because Rufus was pretty smart and pretty human.

MR. TERHORST: Kaiser was there when you took over wasn't he?

MR. POWELL: Yes. They started rotating them, which is probably a good idea I guess, but it meant you had to learn a new group as they came in. There were two or three during the campaign and then two or three that ran the operation during the White House years, so you had to pick up on and get to understand them better.

MR. TERHORST: The secret service is really organized like any police organization, in a very military fashion. Unless you got along well with the White House chief of the secret service detail, your life would be very tough.

MR. POWELL: So they expect, and I guess they have to, that the institutions they come in contact with will also operate in that fashion. And if there's a group that does not operate that way it's the reporters and press people. They forget their tags and they show up late; they want to go around this way and they want to cut across and that sort of thing. When that sort of thing comes up, the only way to get it done is say, ah, come on I'll walk across with him or I'll send Carolyn over there with him. Can't you let him just go there?

MR. REEDY: Yet on the other hand, Rufus once admitted to me that the secret service likes to have a lot of reporters around the President. They figure if any shooting starts it's going to hit them and not him.

MR. THOMPSON: Is fifty too much and thirty too small or are the numbers about right? Is the organization right and the plans for your briefing about right?

MR. TERHORST: The number of people who show up you mean?

QUESTION: The number of people who show up.

MR. REEDY: You mean the journalists?

MR. THOMPSON: Yes, and for your people to get your work done. Is the organization, the numbers part in the management of the office about right?

MR. POWELL: I made a mistake by cutting the staff down considerably. It took me a while to manage to sneak it back up to a reasonable level.

QUESTION: You cut back from what it had been before?

MR. POWELL: Yes, and it was a mistake.

MR. TERHORST: But that wasn't you. You were carrying out a presidential dictum as I understand it. The idea was to get rid of this huge, big White House staff and so you had to do your part.

MR. POWELL: If I had argued about it a lot, I could have been less zealous in my compliance. You can always hide a body somewhere.

MR. REEDY: One of the legacies of Pierre Salinger—and I think it was a reasonably important legacy—was that Pierre had set the thing up in such a way that the White House press staff was not too big when I took over. It didn't have to be because he'd established the type of relationship where you could call the staffs in the Pentagon, the State Department and all over the federal government. That way you, in effect, had a huge staff. But it didn't show up that way in the payroll.

MR. TERHORST: But you know something was said earlier about the care and feeding of the press. Jody mentioned it and George in a sense. When I first started covering the White House, we had that doggone little diplomatic reception room. Anybody who came in to see the President literally had to walk the gauntlet of the press to get in. And then we just sat around waiting, like whatever you want to call it—I suppose somebody would call it jackals—until they came out and then we pounced on them, on the President's guests. We elicited whatever we could out of them before they escaped our clutches and went to their cars and took off. We had little standup booths and that little tiny room, phones on the wall. But you should go in there today and see what the Nixon operation created! They decided that if they couldn't give us any good news, at least they'd take care of us physically. So they covered over the swimming pool that Lyndon made famous and put in two tiers of a huge press room, with a nice lounge and decorated it in modern California style with leather couches; reporters had individual booths with chairs to sit at little desks. And the important wires and the networks had glassed-in booths with doors that closed so you couldn't hear. You had a little private office, courtesy of the government. They took good care of the press, physically.

MR. POWELL: Which goes to show. If you talk to anybody, and I'd be willing to bet they brought it up this time, you [the Miller Center] must have gotten complaints about the horrible working conditions, all cruddy. A reporter would say I've got this little carrel like the one I used to have when I was in graduate school.

MR. TERHORST: Furnished like a dentist's office.

MR. POWELL: We've got four of us trying to crowd in the ABC booth all trying to do our stuff at one time and I've never trusted her anyway, she's always looking over my shoulder. . . .

MR. REEDY: Jerry, for the sake of the record you should have added that when we really didn't want the press to waylay guests they left by the western entrance.

MR. TERHORST: Of course, and they still do today.

MR. POWELL: But there are always those that you didn't want to talk to the press but you couldn't come right out and tell them that you didn't want them to talk to the press. So then you've got the game of how you convince them that one traditionally leaves by West Executive Avenue, that it is indeed the departure point of honor. If anybody of any importance sees the President, he always goes out this door.

QUESTION: How about currying favors with the Presidents' wives?

MR. REEDY: You have to realize—I don't know how it was in other White Houses—that was a completely separate setup with Johnson. When I was there, Mrs. Johnson had Liz Carpenter and she had a rather large staff. There was no sure way of getting at the first lady. I knew her fairly well because I had worked with Johnson for so many years before that. She was surrounded by a rather large staff.

QUESTION: But that wasn't true with the others?

MR. REEDY: I don't know if it was or not.

MR. POWELL: I think every first lady has had a decent size staff of her own.

MR. REEDY: Actually before that I think it was Mrs. Kennedy who first had a staff. Mrs. Kennedy was really the one who started a separate press staff for the first lady. I think Nixon started these huge staffs for the White House press office. I remember having the White House underground that was still there counting the number of heads for me. It's the only way you can find out how many people are in the White House. Nixon had three times as many as I had. But he did not have the same arrangements with the other agencies. So I'm not saying he didn't need them. Just a different setup.

MR. TERHORST: Betty Ford was of course an unusual person. She used to brag about "Well, you know, I have a little influence with the President." I think she popularized the phrase "pillow talk." But she never got herself involved in governmental decisions during the Ford presidency. She tended to stick to her side of the building; she had social functions to take care of and that's a very demanding job. It's not easy to go through what the first lady has to go through. I mean she's either going to make out well or she's going to be sneered at in the paper the next day by all the arbiters of social grace, both as to the nature of the guest list and how they behaved and how she herself might have behaved. I don't recall that Betty Ford was an integral part of that government at all. Perhaps Rosalyn Carter was more a part of the government because she spent so much time campaigning with Jimmy during the campaign. But even if she didn't, they had lunch every day, not every day but a couple of times a week.

MR. POWELL: I had known Mrs. Carter for a long time and had always gotten along very well with her and I'm a great admirer of hers. And it never was particularly a question of access but the Carters were extremely close and still are. They talked to one another about the things that they were doing as I suppose most husbands and wives do. You come home and say well, such and such. She didn't participate as far as decisionmaking was concerned; but you never know what role somebody plays. I suppose you have to sit there in the evening after supper and know when he talked over this or that problem, to know whether what she said had influence on him or not. But in the one area where her influence was directed, it was formally part of the process, that was in political matters. She had great political judgment, which the President respected and which I did, too, and I think everybody else that came to know her did. So in preparing for, say, a political strategy session, you knew that on most occasions Mrs. Carter would be there, would play an active role in discussing whatever was on the agenda. I dealt with her in much the same way that I did any other participant in that meeting in the sense that you usually do a little talking around ahead of time; you try ideas out and see what people think of it. You may, if you have something that you particularly want to push, attempt to build some coalition support ahead of time. She obviously was not just another person around that table. But it was closer to that than anything else.

Plus, there's a sort of indefinable thing there that was always considered in a relationship with her to be an asset. She knew better than anybody else what the President thought, how he was feeling, not so much in specifics, but what might be bothering him that he hadn't mentioned yet and so forth. And if she felt like somebody needed to know, then she'd tell you about it. It was another way for me to understand what my boss is about which is I think something that with every President, every White House staff member has to deal with. It is knowing what the man at the top is thinking and where he's headed and what's eating at him today or even the simple physical things, he is really tired, he's worn out. That is a good thing to know. If a President won't tell you that himself and before it gets to the point that it's obvious that he can't put one foot in front of the other then you can sit down with the schedule and say let's lighten up here and see if we can't give the guy the chance to catch his breath.

MR. REEDY: Lady Bird was rather self-effacing in the White House which I think was really unfortunate for Johnson. Johnson had a peculiar personality. I remember Sam Rayburn talking about a young congressman one day saying, "The damn fool's brilliant but he ain't got no sense." And to a certain extent that described Johnson; he was a very brilliant man but he didn't have much sense. Lady Bird had an awful lot of sense. During the period that he was a senator, he would ultimately bring certain very difficult problems to her and although her solution may never have been brilliant, it was always sensible. I have a feeling he didn't do much of that in the White House, that she did not have quite the same role that she had had during the Senate years. I think it showed up.

QUESTION: Can family ever be a negative factor? I've thought of that in the debate. Amy and the bomb would have been something one certainly would have talked about around the family table, and yet the nation isn't a family. I wondered whether that's an example that things that seem to be worked out in the family sometimes on a public scale, in contrast to a private scale, may not work as well.

MR. POWELL: Family generally ends up being a net debit for every politician. The ideal situation is to find you a guy to work for that's an orphan.

MR. TERHORST: Has no living relatives.

MR. POWELL: No living relatives of any description.

MR. REEDY: I disagree because of Earl Warren. I think Earl Warren's family was a tremendous asset to him. I think that where the family really becomes an asset is that people have the feeling—and I believe they are right about it—that when you look at a man's wife and look at his kids you get some judgment of the man himself, that he's bound to have made an impact on them.

MR. POWELL: The good things that a family does for a President you don't think about because they just happen. But there are always a few that will create problems as you go along, and they are the hardest ones to deal with when they involve family members because it's a family matter in addition to being public.

MR. REEDY: You know I think most people want the first lady to be good. I think they approach her with a rather sympathetic aspect. And she's about the only degree of class that we have in the government. We don't have a queen.

QUESTION: And she didn't ask to be there.

MR. REEDY: She didn't ask to be there but nevertheless she's there. She is the model. They may not imitate the model but at least she's the model of what they think they should respect. There's a very peculiar factor here that's difficult to put your finger on but I think it's terribly important.

MR. TERHORST: I can only recall one time when Mrs. Ford ever got herself involved in a potential news story that turned out it didn't work. Early on Jack Anderson called and wanted the birth dates of all the Ford kids and he said they were checking to see if they had all registered for the draft. Well, of course one was already married and had two kids. Young Steve was about six months away from having a birthday at which he'd have to register. Time went on and I didn't think any more about it. And I got this call one day from Betty Ford at the White House. I was in the White House then and she said, "Jerry, you won't believe what happened but Steve's birthday was two days ago, as you know (because they'd had a birthday party), and he just told me that he hadn't registered. Do you think that's going to get out? Can you keep it from getting out?" I said, "Has he registered now?" "Yes, he registered this morning; we made sure of that." I said, "Well, I'm certainly not going to go out and volunteer it, but if somebody asks me I'll have to tell them the fact that yes, he is registered and if they ask me when I'll tell them when. I won't try to link it, I won't even mention his birthday." Strangely Jack Anderson forgot all about it and it never came up. About three months later there was just a little piece about famous sons who were having trouble with the draft and some of them were questioning whether they should register or not and the story included a line that Steve Ford had registered two days after his birthday, he had said, under parental pressure. The poor kid just forgot to get himself over there. He wasn't questioning whether he should have registered or not, but that was the way it was reported.

QUESTION: Coming off center stage for each one of you, and certainly you've been on it during your time, could each one of you comment on how difficult it is or maybe it isn't, going back to private life and being out of the limelight?

MR. REEDY: Difficult? The one thing that I wanted to do was to get out of that place. I didn't want to get into it and I did want to get out. I never liked it.

MR. POWELL: I would have preferred to leave at a time under circumstances of my own choosing. The only thing I miss is the access to information and I never really thought about it so much while I was there but that ability to pick up a phone and get those folks that you were talking about in short order in Defense or State or Labor or Health and Human Services or wherever you want them and get pretty much the best information that the American government has available to it on anything that's going on anywhere in the world, just out of being nosy. Curiously, it's a heck of a thing when all of a sudden you realize those people are not going to respond to you in quite the same way. The thing I don't miss is as my wife says, that everything she despised about Washington, she no longer has to put up with any more.

MR. REEDY: I knew that it was going to break up my relationship with Johnson, which it did. I'd had a very close relationship with him for about ten or twelve years. I knew that was going to go down the drain, which was inevitable. And I knew that what it would actually do, instead of putting me in the center of the political spectrum that sooner or later I'd get shoved to the side because of the way he wanted the press secretary to operate. It was not the way I could operate.

MR. TERHORST: I'm like Jody—I left at the time and place of my own choosing, but not under the circumstances that I wanted. I must say I did like being there. I liked it—I suppose every reporter has some sort of inner craving that if you cover a building as I had for about twelve or fifteen years then you really like to know what goes on behind the scenes (and is it true that the reasons these briefings are late is because everybody's sitting around drinking coffee and kibitzing and not really working?). Well, I soon disabused myself of a lot of impressions, including that one. I never worked so hard in my life as I did during my time in the White House. So I enjoyed it from the standpoint that Jody mentioned, being able to talk to people and getting answers at the highest possible levels when you needed them, from the President on down, having a sense—and it's a nice sense too—of being able hopefully in a good way, to influence the shape of the news as well as just being an observer of a happening or a reporter of a happening. I can also say there was a lot of relief in not being there after I did leave. I don't know how Jody stood it for four years or George as long as he did because there's tremendous pressure. Not just time and physical pressure but mental pressure. I don't think I've ever been in a situation where it reminded me more of being in World War II in the Pacific in the Marine Corps. Just the sheer, honest-to-God unrelenting, unremitting, seven day a week, twenty-four hour a day pressure to be on top of that particular assignment. It's wearing. I'm very glad to have that off my back.

MR. REEDY: Well, the worst part of it is the job. As a job it is really rather easy—if you could only do it without Presidents.

MR. TERHORST: Or the press.

MR. REEDY: It's easier to handle the press than it is to handle Presidents. You've got certain alternates, but that really is the rough part of it. The fact that what you are supposed to do, or what you should be doing I think is a relatively simple job, but the complications is that you're torn between two different visions, the press on one side and the President on the other side. You have some sympathy for both of them if you have any sense because they're both kind of right and both wrong at the same time. That's one of the reasons my heart is still back in the Senate when it comes to Washington. I'm a Senate type.

MR. POWELL: Let's face it, too. You do, although you very seldom admit it, deep down inside like to think on occasion that you did something that helped something good to happen. Even though, if you look at it objectively, you realize that at best your influence, if positive, was also marginal. But you say, well, maybe if I hadn't done a decent job on this or that particular issue or this or that particular briefing or wherever, things might not have turned out right. At the very least you can say I had it within my power to screw it up royally and I didn't, and that is not necessarily something that you miss so much as this is something that you certainly, if you're honest with yourself, look back on and say, well, I'm glad I had a chance to do that. And you probably miss it on occasion. I find myself every now and then thinking, I wish I had a chance to get my bore in on this or that as I see something moving along and another White House is going to have to deal with it and I'd like to take my shot at it, sitting around a table before they decide what they're going to do.

MR. REEDY: I have a feeling for what you describe but only with respect to the Senate Democratic Policy Committee when I was staff director. There I can look back with same feeling of accomplishment. As far as I was concerned the White House was not a very splendid misery.

MR. THOMPSON: One of the things that impressed me when we met with the three senior White House reporters was precisely on this issue of doing something worthwhile; there seemed to be a little asymmetry. I wonder whether it's at all related to the tone of the discussions of the two groups. Whether it was the cubicles or being herded together like cattle or whatever it was, there was a sense of hostility, bitterness, disappointment, and frustration on the part of the reporters we met with and it kept coming out. They defined their job as the search for truth; so do we at the university, we say that the scholarship is the unending search for some kind of truth. But we have years and years to do it and they have twenty-four hours. Maybe there is no such thing as truth, perhaps for either group, but certainly it's hard to do it in twenty-four hours.

There is a fellow who's written a lot on leadership named Bob Greenleaf in Boston who says there are two types in the world, conceptualizers and doers. Historically, business and government have worked when one didn't try to do the other's job or imagined that they could do the job of the other; the growth of the railroad industry, the communications industry is identifiable with keeping those two groups separate and maximizing the strengths of either one. In a curious way we almost felt when we were talking to some of the reporters that they felt they were better doers than some of you were, that some of your mistakes might not have been mistakes they would have made as doers. It's too long a way of asking the question, I know, but there's something about the atmosphere of the two discussions that I'm not sure I can explain, but I do feel there's a difference and I wonder if you have any idea why there should be that difference.

MR. REEDY: Different view of the world is what there is. Journalists, reporters, and politicians see a different world, literally. The politician is brought up in the adversarial world. When Clausewitz said that war is politics carried on by other means, he had the thing exactly reversed. Politicians have the same attitude toward life that a general has: they have friends and they have enemies and they have people that are too stupid to know they're going to become friends or enemies. Journalists see a somewhat different world. I'm not saying which is right or which is wrong. But things that seem perfectly obvious and perfectly ordinary to the politician do not seem perfectly obvious and do not seem perfectly normal to the reporter and vice versa. I also wish reporters would stop dealing in truth. You know Plato had trouble determining truth; I rather question the qualification of a three hundred dollar a week reporter to determine what is truth. What they deal in is facts, which is a somewhat different thing.

QUESTION: I wonder if Plato got a good salary?

MR. TERHORST: One of the things I think there's a misconception about, among my former colleagues in the press, that is this business on truth. They often make the mistake of equating truth with news. News and truth are not the same. Never have been. What can be newsy may turn out later to have been false, but at the time it occurred it was newsy and therefore made the papers or made television. This is a hard concept for people in the press to think about. I know why they do it. I know why I always charged myself up. I was going to get the truth and going to get to the bottom of this thing. I was going to write it truthfully. I was going to get truthful answers. If it didn't come out right, chances were it wasn't my fault, not because I might have asked stupid questions but because perhaps somebody was being evasive with me and not telling me the truth.

There is the adversarial thing that goes on between the press and governmental people, and I think it's particularly acute at the White House, just because of the way the two sides come together. There's very little time for genuine camaraderie or what Jody was telling you about, or sitting down over a lunch like we had today and just discussing an issue without confrontational kinds of questioning, prosecutorial kinds of questioning, did you or did you not do this? If you did this, why did you do that? What was behind it? There is a heavy atmosphere of suspicion that somebody is trying, in a word, to screw somebody someplace or the American people. In this part of the process, I have often wished that the press would deal with the government like lawyers in a courtroom deal with each other. They can be very mean and tough to each other. Politicians can be very mean and tough to each other on the floor of the Senate. And one may win and one may lose, but they don't necessarily go out of there with a chip on their shoulder. They don't remain enemies.

MR. REEDY: You raise a very important point there.

MR. TERHORST: This attitude bothers me, among some of my fellows. Not all of them have it but some of them do.

MR. REEDY: Jerry, there's a certain distinction you have to make. When I covered the Senate as a newsman I could get into a fight with a senator and we'd scream at each other all day long and in the evening we might meet at the bar and have a quiet drink and be friends. The reason was that I was only interested in what he did as a senator. One of the problems here is that the press is not just interested in what the President does as President. They are interested in the President as a person, which means that there is no point at which there can be a natural, relaxed relationship between a reporter and a President. That is not possible.

MR. TERHORST: I don't think it should be either.

MR. REEDY: One is being taken into camp by the other, if there is such a relationship. Now, what that means is that it extends to the whole White House staff. And I think this accounts for part of the bitterness. Every President that I've ever heard of always feels that he's surrounded by eyes that are trying to watch him every time he goes to the toilet and in a sense he's right. I think one of the most revealing things to me was when Luci Baines decided that she was better off going to school in Washington, D.C. than going down to the University of Texas because she'd watched Lynda Bird at Texas who had to have the secret service agents sleep outside the dormitory door every night. And Luci had figured out that the only place you could get any privacy was in the White House. And that's true. All Presidents eventually—everyone I've ever heard of—got the feeling that he was beleaguered, and that is bound to spread to the staff. I think in a sense he is.

MR. POWELL: Well, as the old saying goes, just because you're paranoid doesn't mean nobody's out to get you. It's much worse for a President though. I may be deluding myself, but I think I had on the whole some pretty good personal relationships. I mean, there was always a degree of separation that I felt was as important for my good as I think the reporters did for theirs. But with most of the people that covered the White House regularly and for most of them I felt I got along alright, despite the fact that I had a fairly hot temper and often got into fairly heated discussions with them and said things to them and about them that they probably didn't much like and they did the same thing to me. So you had Frank Cormier. I remember coming back, from the Middle East with old Frank and I have never had anybody more upset with me. Frank is a pretty mild mannered sort of fellow for the most part and a real gentleman, and he was so upset with me and had all sorts of unkind things to say. And if it hadn't been because I felt so good because we had the treaty, I probably would have been as offensive myself. I don't know if Frank has completely forgiven me yet for what he thought I did to him at the time. But I don't think it affected us two days later. This was a conversation that lasted from Cairo to the Azores, but after it was over it was over. We had certainly said in that length of time everything we had to say on both sides of the issues. So far as I know that was the end of it. I'm sure if things like this came up again we'd probably pick up right where we left off without much more enlightenment on either side.

MR. REEDY: No, but I doubt if the argument would be as bitter now, Jody. What I mean is that you're no longer in that relationship.

MR. POWELL: Sure. But I mean even at that time, even with the arguments and the fights, you can under certain circumstances, if things aren't too nasty, leave it there and go have a drink.

MR. TERHORST: There's something else, though. I think we're all aware of it, three of us anyway are, and that is the change that has come over that White House press room in recent years. It was always pretty tough, George, when you were there. I can remember throwing some pretty tough questions at you and everybody else did, too. But it wasn't venomous, there wasn't a meanness to the attitude. During the Nixon years, there was a mean confrontational period in the White House press room, absolutely total distrust by the press of what was being said, derisive laughter and answers, snickers, a lot of baiting mainly for the purpose of just baiting, not to get news. You never saw the results of the baiting in the stories. Some of that has hung over. There are people like Lester Kinsolving in this world and a few others who seem to think that their whole calling is to create a scene in the press room. Yet very few of them ever write about it. They don't even use it. I don't know why they put themselves through the exercise.

MR. POWELL: It's become sort of ritualized in a way, the debating still goes on, but I think press secretaries have learned that it really doesn't make any difference.

MR. TERHORST: It poisons the atmosphere though. You can't hold a serious news conference.

MR. POWELL: It detracts from trying. If anything takes more than about two minutes to explain, you'll have a hard time doing it on occasion if you've got one of the dingbos there that's going to jump up and say, well, what about. . . ?

MR. REEDY: I don't think Watergate is the sole explanation for it although I think it is important. I think that Watergate crystallized a lot of feelings. I think that to a certain extent one of the things that is happening here is there is an increasing remoteness of the President. And I think that to a certain extent the press feels some of this remoteness. I covered some of the Roosevelt press conferences in the closing days and it was rather a wonderful thing. There would be five or six of us standing around his desk. We could ask questions and if we didn't like the answers, we could ask more questions. Of course we wouldn't like those answers, either. Roosevelt was a master at handling questions. He loved it. He did this twice a week. And under Harry Truman, the press conferences got a lot bigger, but there was still a personal sort of a relationship between Harry and many members of the press. But in recent years there has been, for all sorts of reasons, including television, which requires the elaborate cameras being set up, forces at work that automatically put a certain chill on the relationship.

QUESTION: Impersonal under those circumstances?

MR. REEDY: Where the television really controls the presidential press conference is through the thirty minute time slot. Maybe a secret service man can't say no to the President but the TV guy can cut him off at the end of thirty minutes or at least he will be cut off. That, plus, I think, the increasing amount of security around the President has had some impact, plus the fact that the White House staff has become so very much larger. When I covered presidential press conferences under Roosevelt, I doubt if the whole staff was more than forty or fifty.

MR. POWELL: And also things tend to feed on themselves. The change in the relationship makes it harder for a President to be as regular, as we were talking about it before. You can't have under present circumstances a relaxed personal sort of relationship between working journalist reporters and a President. When you all were standing around covering Roosevelt, you also operated within somewhat better, whether you consider them better or not, or at least different generally understood standards and rules of behavior. You couldn't herd them in there now twice a week.

MR. REEDY: It's impossible.

MR. POWELL: Even if you could get them all in there.

MR. REEDY: Theodore Roosevelt had a rather close personal relationship with certain favored reporters. (There's been quite a bit of literature on this.) And he would see them in the White House and he would give them stories. But those reporters always obeyed Theodore Roosevelt's injunctions as to conditions under which the story could be written. There you did have a close relationship. But again that was because the particular reporters with whom he had the relationship were not independent of Theodore Roosevelt. They got cut off real fast if they did not play by his rules.

MR. POWELL: Well, Kennedy was the last President to have anything like that.

MR. REEDY: And even his was really not with working journalists. It was certain journalists. You know, most journalists are kind of frustrated intellectuals and he had them pretty well spotted.

MR. POWELL: Frustrated advisers to the prince.

MR. REEDY: Right.

MR. THOMPSON: We touched on this earlier, but in retrospect and ideally what would be the perfect background for the press secretary if you weren't chosen as randomly as at the court of Louis

XIV, as you've mentioned several times today. If you could pick the perfect person to be the President's press secretary, what would his background be?

MR. REEDY: A friend of the President.

MR. POWELL: Ronald Reagan.

MR. REEDY: No. What you would do is see who is closest to the President, that's what you need.

QUESTION: Despite his background?

MR. REEDY: That doesn't matter as long as he's literate.

MR. POWELL: It certainly would help to have a background in journalism and to have been a working reporter. I can say that as one who never was. I managed to get by but I would have been better off.

MR. REEDY: I think you got by better than some who weren't.

MR. POWELL: There are a lot of things to figure into it, but, all things being equal, there's no doubt that to have a sense of what these other people are doing, are dealing with and what helps them and hurts them and makes life easier or more difficult and how they're likely to respond helps because you have done it and reacted to those things yourself. It is an asset. It can also be, for some people, I think, a problem and I saw it not in myself but in dealing with the people that we hired to work in the press office and to be spokesmen or women in the various departments. Some of them, most of them did come out of journalism, at least at some point in their career. Some of them who came right out of journalism were excellent and did tremendous jobs and I think enjoyed it for the most part. I think Tom Ross at Defense, for example, did a great job. Others had a hard time crossing the line. And it was more difficult for them because they were in a new role but in the same place. They were dealing with their old friends, drinking buddies and partners in crime but in a totally different situation. Differences that were bitter and difficult enough on a professional level took on a personal aspect. It became not only "How could this bastard do this to me?" but it became, "How could this bastard do this who has been in my house and bounced my children on his knee? I remember the time I saved his rear end when he was too drunk to file and I filed for him. Now he's doing this to me!" I never had that to deal with because I didn't know these people well enough to have that network of relationships.

MR. TERHORST: There's an element of truth in that because I still do have some good friends in the press corps, but to a great degree that friendship went on hold while I was in the White House.

MR. POWELL: And it works the other way. Reporters, I'm sure, feel how could this guy do this to me?

90

MR. TERHORST: On both sides there was an estrangement. I had to guard my tongue so that I wouldn't unnecessarily give them a break on something. I mean, I couldn't sit down and discuss the situation with them as we might have been able to do before. On the other hand, they also, I think, felt a little awkward in asking me some questions for fear that perhaps maybe they were straining a friendship. It is touchy; there's no doubt about that.

MR. REEDY: You know you get back to one basic thing, though. A lot of things might be helpful. As I said literacy, ability to read—that sort of thing. But they are only helpful. What really counts is whether he has the President's confidence. If he doesn't have the President's confidence, I don't care who you put in there, it's not going to work.

MR. THOMPSON: We wanted to make you feel right at home so there may or may not be some television cameras outside the door as you come out.

MR. POWELL: Who do you want to go out on West Executive?

MR. THOMPSON: Thank you, messrs. press secretaries.

THE WHITE HOUSE, THE MEDIA AND THE MAN IN THE MIDDLE

George E. Reedy

It is something of a paradox that the office of White House press secretary is at the same time one of the most frequently analyzed and least understood posts in the American government. Almost everyone who has held the job has said to himself, after reading the voluminous works upon the subject, "They sure aren't talking about me!"

The phenomenon arises out of varying perceptions. Most of us see the world in terms of institutions we already understand and when we come across something which is outside the pattern of our everyday existence we try to force it into the pattern rather than change the pattern itself. The unhappy lot of the White House press secretary arises from the fact that the position *is* unique and therefore everyone assigns to him a role which he really cannot play.

Presidents, or at least those I have been able to see at close range, regard the position as a super-duper public relations post whose mission is to build a favorable image of the Chief Executive. The press, which I have been able to observe closely for a much longer period, believes that the assignment *should* be to act as a legman digging up stories for White House correspondents. Cabinet officers probe constantly to determine whether the press secretary will serve as a pathway to confidential sessions with the President. Politicians outside the administration believe him to be the director of vast plots to brainwash the public. And private citizens have mixed emotions including, quite often, the feeling that he is a publicity hound who hogs too much television time. It is all rather bewildering.

It reality, the White House press office cannot serve any of those purposes without jeopardizing the one role in which it can perform a truly useful service for the President. That service is to act as a point of contact between the President and the press—a point of contact which is vital in a society which operates best when there is a continuing flow of information. The jobs which the press secretary should perform well are to speak for the President when he is not there to speak for himself and to make the necessary arrangements so the press—which ultimately means the public—will have adequate access to the President.

Eisenhower/Hagerty as models

Unfortunately, only one White House press secretary was given full scope to perform the job in this fashion and it may be of some significance that he initiated most of the press office practices which continue to be viable to this day. I am referring to the late Jim Hagerty. He had the good fortune to serve Dwight D. Eisenhower who had learned in the Army the staff and command system under which generals turned responsibilities over to their subordinates and left them alone as long as they did well what they were supposed to do. Jim knew his business and Ike never had to intervene.

The basic principle which guided Hagerty was to sustain the credibility of the Press Office at all costs. He was well aware of the ephemeral quality of that credibility and how quickly it could vanish if he indulged in public relations "tricks." This did not prevent Jim from presenting Eisenhower in the most favorable light possible. He beat the drums loudly whenever an event reflected favorably upon the President and became very straight-faced when he was down-playing unfortunate realities. But he did not conceal those realities and he would give a straight answer to a straight question.

Other press secretaries would have liked to follow the Hagerty model. Unfortunately, they worked for Presidents who had no intention of following the *Eisenhower* model for conducting press relations. Instead, they looked upon the press as an instrument which could be used to create a favorable picture of the Chief Executive and make him invincible and beloved in the hearts of the electorate. It is obvious that most Presidents have held this view and I worked for one who carried it to extreme ends.

LBJ's PR-view of press secretaries

I have a vivid memory of Lyndon B. Johnson telling Pierre Salinger: "You elected President Kennedy!" It was a remark partly intended as a cut at me (I had just given him some advice he did not like) and partly intended to flatter Pierre. But it still reflected the Johnsonian belief that the press secretary was a "PR" man which meant he was akin to a high priest who possessed arcane knowledge that could ensure perpetual "good" press play and therefore perpetual reelection. Pierre was a thoroughly competent professional who had done an excellent job for Kennedy and he found it difficult to conceal his amusement over the LBJ naivete.

The reality of the situation is that the White House press secretary can do even less in manipulating the press than the President can do. The Chief Executive may *delegate* some manipulative powers to the secretary (although it is an unwise delegation) but the subordinate can make only a limited use of them. To understand this fully, it is necessary to consider the presidential powers.

Actually, it is *not* difficult for a President to manipulate the press provided that he recognizes the *limitations* of what can be done by such manipulation and provided *also* that he recognizes the nature of the levers that are available to him. They are *not* the techniques that are so successful in the field of commercial public relations. Instead, they are related directly to the President's capacity to generate action in our society and that means to generate news.

TR, FDR, JFK . . .
They understood the press

There have been three Presidents in this century—the period in which White House press relations became crucial—who truly understood the working of the press. They were the two Roosevelts—Theodore and Franklin D.—and John F. Kennedy. These three did not rely upon gimmicks or stunts, although they were blessed with personalities which made them attractive to journalists. Instead, they recognized the potency of headlines as a *political* instrument which could not, under any circumstances, be wielded by opponents with the same ease as the man in the Oval Office. They wasted no time in promoting "favorable" stories (although they got plenty of them without even trying) but concentrated their efforts on timing the flow of presidential announcements to keep themselves center stage, when that was a commanding tactical position to hold, and to put someone else there whenever the audience (meaning the electorate) worked itself into a mood to throw tomatoes, dead cats and brickbats.

What really made these three Presidents effective as press manipulators, however, was that they operated through tactics which did not make them vulnerable to damaging charges of manipulation. What they were doing was feeding the press legitimate stories *which the press would want to carry anyway* but doling them out at times and under circumstances which suited the political plans of the Presidents. Journalists could not charge that news was being withheld; only that its release was adapted to White House convenience. This does not sound like a very impressive point to the general public which can become aroused only when there is convincing evidence that news has been manufactured, distorted or withheld altogether.

TR's gospel for "using" the press

Virtually all the effective techniques of "using" the press for political purposes were worked out by Theodore Roosevelt—probably because he was the first President to grasp the fundamental role of the media in the communications between leaders and the electorate when society has become massive and somewhat impersonal. Basically, these techniques can be categorized as follows:

● To use the commanding position of the presidency to generate headlines which would make the Chief Executive appear to be the prime mover of all the major currents in society.

● To use that same commanding position to smother the opposition in a deluge of headlines which would crowd dissenters off the front page.

● To play upon the competitive desire of all journalists by selecting susceptible individuals to float "trial balloons"—anonymous stories about forthcoming policy initiatives which could then be embraced or denied publicly, depending upon public reaction. (Actually, this is a form of market research much more effective than anything that a polling organization can offer.)

● To feed the yearning of White House correspondents for "inside dope" by "leaking" stories which put opponents in an unfavorable light without branding the President as a churl resorting to mean, personal attacks upon his political antagonists.

Of course, there are variations upon these four basic themes. There are times when a President might want to put someone else on stage center to become associated with policies that might turn out badly. Franklin Delano Roosevelt was very good at hedging his chancier bets by allowing associates just enough spotlight to dilute the blame should things go wrong. I have a strong suspicion that Ronald Reagan has mastered the same art, simply because I have no other explanation for the extent to which this obviously astute political operator has permitted low level subordinates to bathe in publicity. Obviously, there is ample elbow room in all four categories for tactical flexibility.

Manipulation . . . and its price

Actually, except for the two Roosevelts and Kennedy (we have still to gather enough evidence for a judgment on Mr. Reagan) none of our other Presidents has made effective use of the weapons available. Lyndon B. Johnson was quite good at keeping himself center stage and, as Senator Barry Goldwater learned in 1964, superb at smothering opposition. (Every time Goldwater charged that U.S. defenses had deteriorated under Democratic administrations, Johnson would declassify the development of a new "super" weapon and that was the end of the argument.) But when it came to floating trial balloons and leaking stories, LBJ was very crude. He used the presidential position to secure trivial "puff pieces" about his modesty and dislike of power (which no one believed) and to play tricks on the press. One of his proudest boasts was that he had trapped newsmen into writing stories that he could *not* produce a budget below $100,000,000,000 when he had a $98,000,000,000 budget already drawn up. He did not tell me what he was doing but I could guess. I could not figure out which was the more juvenile act—the silly game he had devised or his bragging about it. All the story did for him was to foster a reputation for trickery which hurt badly when the going got really rough.

Obviously, there is a price to be paid for the employment of manipulative techniques even when they are handled skillfully. Men and women do not like to be "used" and sooner or later press resentment develops against the user. Of course, there is nothing that journalists can do about it as long as the White House is careful to resort only to legitimate news—a commodity which it has in great quantities. No correspondent will find a sympathetic ear for a complaint that he was fed a top story to suit the convenience of the President. But impotence to respond only makes things more galling. It is no accident that Harry S. Truman who did not use any of the classic tactics was probably the President who, in my memory, enjoyed the highest degree of personal popularity with the presidential reporters. Unfortunately, it should be added that he also had the worst press, even though Richard M. Nixon might dispute that statement.

Presidents and reporters . . . a running warfare

It does not tell the *whole* story, however, to state that the press lacks power to counter the ploys of the presidential manipulation artists. Individual reporters cannot turn down important stories tossed into their laps. But they can set out on a search for facts which are embarrassing and for contrary opinions which can be woven into their accounts. What this means is that sooner or later there will be a counterweight to provide balance and out of which the public at large will benefit. The real safeguard for adequate communications in a free society may well be the bruised egos of journalists who want to prove to themselves that they are something other than megaphones for the man in the Oval Office. Without that factor, I would be very pessimistic over the fate of our society should we ever acquire a Chief Executive with an even higher degree of artfulness than the two Roosevelts and Kennedy.

Underlying the whole process, of course, is a very simple fact which most commentators have failed to grasp—probably because it is *too* simple. It is that Presidents *are* politicans and politicians will *always* see the press as an arena for warfare. The concept that a newspaper or a television news presentation exists to foster the political dialogue in a free society is incomprehensible to the political mind. In a lifetime of observing politicians—from the ward level in Chicago when I was a child to the White House when I was fully mature—one aspect of their personalities has been consistent. It is that all of them believed that stories were written to advance or retard a cause—not because something had happened.

This factor is at the root of the running warfare that has characterized the relations between the press and the presidency since the days of George Washington. It is a warfare which has varied in intensity but only Gerald Ford seems to have been totally free of it. (This may well be because he was appointed—not elected. The election process is a ritual of anointment as well as selection.) The basic problem is that politicians and journalists literally see different worlds. The politician classifies people in terms of friend or foe and sees no reason to exempt reporters from such classification. The journalist classifies people in terms of those "who tell it straight" and those "who tell it crooked" and the journalist cannot accept the reasoning of the partisan that whatever advances a "noble" cause is the "straight way" of telling the story. These differing viewpoints promote an adversary relationship which intensifies in proportion to the degree of honesty held by the participants. The theme song of the White House press room should be a parody of Kipling's "East is East and West is West and never the twain shall meet . . ."

News unsatisfactory? Kill the messenger!

This is the milieu in which the press secretary operates. He has no authority to speak in any manner other than that which the President would speak—and he would be faithless to his trust if he did so. (After all, no one elected him to speak for the United States—only for the President.) Therefore, to the press he must appear as an adversary seeking to promote a partisan cause. On the other hand, he has no authority to dictate the tenor of the daily news report. Therefore, to the President he will eventually appear as an incompetent, unless he becomes an expert in feeding the presidential paranoia (it always develops) about newspaper conspiracies against the White House. Occasionally, of course, there is a President like Eisenhower who really does leave things to his subordinates or like Franklin D. Roosevelt who commands his own press operation. In either of these cases, the press secretary's life can be idyllic.

Unfortunately such Presidents are rare. For most press secretaries the choice presented is that of taking the President's side and holding the job but just becoming a press pariah (often quite unfairly) or taking the side of the press and being displaced after a suitable period. Of course, should there be a President who is very naive about press relations, it might be possible to convince him that the secretary is fighting a gallant battle against the press and then convince the press that the press secretary is fighting a gallant battle to bring them the news. Barnum said, "There's one born every minute," and on some questions both politicians and journalists can exhibit an incredible degree of gullibility.

These matters are worth consideration—not because there is any need to sympathize with press secretaries but because the considerations illuminate the fundamental problems of the office. In technical terms it is not a difficult job, however nerve wracking it may be to speak under circumstances where such dire consequences can flow from a slip of the tongue. All that is required is a reasonable amount of intelligence; a reasonable amount of responsibility; and a reasonable amount of understanding of the technical problems of the press. It is conceivable, of course, that a press secretary could also be a policy adviser to the President in which case he *should* have qualities above the average. But he would be an adviser only as a sideline. The press operation of the White House *does not call for a policy office.*

This is a point which is understood by a very few members of the press. Many journalists have a view of the press secretary as the equivalent to a minister of information—a position quite common among certain types of nations under parliamentary governments. Therefore, they look to the press secretary to produce stories for them—overlooking the fact that the right to produce also implies the right not to produce. It would be well if journalists knew more about ministers of information. Most of them exist in countries where there is a degree of control over the press. They have the authority to *release* information but they have equal authority to *withhold* information. Of course, in our society officials can also withhold information but should the press dig it up anyway they can do nothing effective to stop publication. A free press does not rest upon press officials but upon digging reporters.

Regardless of philosophies, however, the press secretary can do nothing but speak for the President and if the President chooses not to speak that ends the matter. The secretary may *advise* speaking but in my experience Presidents—and I am not referring only to Johnson— are not prone to take advice they do not want. It is at this point that life in the press office becomes stormy. Many of the White House correspondents will be well aware that their troubles trace back to the President. But they cannot reach him, except during press conferences where they are too busy asking "news" questions to register complaints. Frustrated men and women must take out their rage on somebody and as a general rule the press secretary is the only available target.

The obstreperous press . . . thank goodness

In recent years, a surprisingly large number of secretaries have had minimal—sometimes non-existent—reporting backgrounds. The natural tendency of people who have spent most of their adult life in public relations or in a government information service is to sympathize with their client. Naturally, they side emotionally, as well as publicly, with the President and what this has produced is the introduction into the public discussion of the phrase "the obstreperous press." In turn, this has heated up the antagonisms between journalists who suspect the entire White House of mendacity (or at least subreption) and White House officials who regard the press corps as a group of sadists who are abusing their privileges under the First Amendment.

In one sense, both groups are right. Presidents *do* mislead— sometimes consciously but more often because they are so convinced of the righteousness of their cause that they are blind to any evidence of virtue on the part of the opposition. Journalists *are* obstreperous—but so is the public which they are supposed to supply with information. In a free society, citizens will *always* be obstreperous and one of the harshest conditions for holding high office is that leaders must put up with the often presumptuous demands of the public. I have often wondered whether the basic reason for the rage expressed by politicians against reporters is that the latter personify the electorate and officials cannot snap back at the electorate.

In terms of peace and serenity, it is unfortunate that more tranquil methods of keeping our society informed cannot be devised. That, however, is a vain hope unless some magic formula can be found to tranquilize society itself. It is true that calmer types of co-existence can be found in the government agencies outside the White House where press officers and correspondents dwell together in considerable harmony. This, however, offers no model which can be imitated by the President. Those agencies are not inherently political even though an administration may use them politically. The correspondents who cover the agencies are primarily interested in their programs and hardly ever seek personal stories about the agency heads—a fact which is a major source of irritation with Presidents. The professional information officers of the government are rarely caught up in the swirl of adversary politics and when they are, the responsibility for calling the shots rests upon the White House in any case.

Desideratum: the press office as service office

Regardless of the problems, the office of White House press secretary will almost certainly continue simply because it fills a requirement of mass society. Some Presidents have toyed with the idea of abolishing it or altering the post beyond recognition. At one point, Johnson laid plans to have a different White House staff member brief the press each day (or whenever he had some news to give out). Some of Mr. Reagan's staff members played with the idea of splitting the job among four briefing experts. Both plans foundered on practical realities. In a mass society, there must be some fixed point to which the press can repair for an authoritative answer to questions and to obtain access to the Chief Executive. Without that fixed point, the press would be lost. It cannot even follow the President through the streets in a parade unless some official is present to pass them through the secret service and police lines. And it certainly cannot get to the President on its own initiative sufficiently often to gain the information that citizens must have to function in a democracy.

When these points are considered, the reasons for isolating the White House press office from the public relations operation becomes obvious. The press office *must be believed* if it to render any service at all and publicity gimmicks do not promote believability. Obviously the President is going to put his best foot forward at any and all times and there is no reason why he should not. Only a candidate for the tooth fairy will expect a politician to do anything other than recommend himself highly. It would be well, however, if the office of the press secretary could be properly defined and recognized for what it should be—a service office for the press, which in turn, means a service office for the public.

THE PRESIDENT AND THE PRESS: STRUGGLE FOR DOMINANCE

George E. Reedy

It was frequently remarked by his associates that Lyndon B. Johnson was the same as any other politician only more so. The basis for this judgment was a persistence and a determination that magnified for the viewer all of his faults and all of his virtues. There were some respects in which he was an extraordinarily subtle man. But once he had embarked on a course of action, he followed through to the end, and the pattern was clearly discernible.

In the field of press relations, he had no subtlety whatsoever. There were individual incidents in which he would baffle journalists. But they were usually instances which resulted in no real value to him other than an opportunity to boast over his ability to catch the press napping. The result was that they were invariably prepared when he repeated a tactic because they had heard from his own lips what he had done and why. When it came to his press strategies, he was the number one leaker in the Lyndon B. Johnson camp—something that he never understood. His success was really due to his rare skill as a political leader and took place despite, rather than because of, his press relations.

Nevertheless, the direct relations between Lyndon B. Johnson and the press are worth considerably more study than they have received. It is probable that they afford some valuable clues to the relations between political leaders and the press generally. In my judgment, he was reacting to the press out of the same considerations which move a majority of politicians. The difference was that most of the others would pull back when a tactic misfired. Johnson would persist even when failure was evident. It was not lack of intelligence on his part, but rather a stronger will.

Partisan View of Press

The basic problem was a view of the press which led him into some strange paths. He regarded newspapers and newscasts as partisan arenas in which contending politicians struggled for an advantage. To a certain extent, of course, this view can be justified. The problem was that he refused to believe that the press had any other function. He was convinced that every news story (with the possible exception of the weather) was printed because it had been inspired by a public relations counsel. He could not believe that anything was set up in type just because it happened.

As a result, every newspaper reference to him was examined painstakingly to determine whether it was favorable or unfavorable. Unfortunately, his concept of favorable was a story carrying flattering adjectives topped by a picture in which his hair was neatly combed, his suit was freshly pressed, and his left profile was prominent. Anything that fell short of this ideal was "unfavorable" and the writer marked down as an enemy. At one time, for example, Helen Thomas of UPI wrote a story on a walk from his ranchhouse to the nearby home of his very colorful Cousin Auriole. It was a warm, human account of the type that usually sends PR men to bed with pleasant dreams. Not so on that one. Helen had written that Cousin Auriole had come to the door in her bare feet and in Lyndon Johnson's mind this was an attack upon his family as being poor, white trash. It took some time for the coldness between the two to thaw.

The more serious problem, however, was that his view of journalism led him to treat journalists as people who had to be bamboozled, bullied, cajoled, or bribed with entertainment. He could not comprehend any business relationship in which he accepted them for what they were and they accepted him for what he was. He thought his attitude toward the press was entirely ethical because in his mind it was what every other political leader was doing and he was merely reacting in self-defense. The fact that he was seldom successful was not regarded by him as evidence that his view was wrong but as evidence that he was not very good at playing the game.

The preferred Lyndon B. Johnson tactic was lavish entertainment. I am not certain, however, that this was solely due to a desire to influence the press. He was a man who liked to entertain lavishly at any time, and newsmen and newswomen were more frequently available for an improptu party than other groups. Some of the long sessions with the press corps in the White House on Saturday morning or at the ranch on weekends were probably traceable to loneliness rather than a desire for publicity. Nevertheless, he would be outraged by any story he deemed to be hostile written by a reporter who had attended one of his soirees. He regarded such items as a breach of good manners.

Closely allied to the entertainment strategy was the implied offer of exclusive stories in return for favorable treatment. He was fond of telling a group of journalists that he would "make big men out of you" leaving them with the impression that he was ready to feed them some rare delicacies in the way of news if they were ready to treat him "right." It is rather interesting that, whereas the entertainment tactic occasionally produced some outrageous puff pieces, the "make big men out of you" usually backfired. It was too direct a challenge to individual integrity, and no one was willing to take it up when stated so boldly.

The most evident Johnson press failures were in the field of psychology. He had read somewhere that people have a tendency to repeat words often used. At one point, he tested this theory in an effort to induce journalists to praise him for his sincerity. For at least two weeks, every sentence in his conversations with the press included the word "sincere." It never worked because sincerity is a quality which reporters usually ascribe to people whom they like but whom they regard as ineffective. They did not put him in that class.

The most effective Johnson tactic during the 1964 campaign was to smother the press with a series of stories which took minds off possibilities of criticism. He was almost constantly on the phone to Secretary of Defense Robert S. McNamara and could produce revelations of new weapons on the drawing board whenever Senator Barry Goldwater, his Republican opponent, would charge him with military weakness. Such announcements came so thick and fast that eventually they appeared to be farcical.

Unfortunately, he ran things into the ground. He refused to leave reporters alone—even for a few minutes. He was convinced that if they were left to their own devices, they would hatch anti-Johnson stories and therefore they had to be kept busy. He made it a practice, for example, to emerge from his cabin and sit with the press pool that accompanied him in the presidential airplane. These pools have a long history. Their function is to assure the national press some presence on the scene in the event that something untoward occurs. The members of the pools are not particularly anxious to write stories. Usually, they would prefer some rest. It was only a short time until the President became a bore, addicted to long, rambling conversations because all the important news had been revealed already.

105

In the beginning of his presidency, Lyndon B. Johnson actually had a "good press." Journalists were fascinated by him and they regarded him as a highly able man. Their stories, at least in my judgment, reflected considerable admiration and even a degree of affection. The poor press which came on later was something that he brought on himself. Incidents, such as those described above, eroded his standing until it was almost nonexistent.

Adversary Role

The major problem, however, was the Lyndon B. Johnson love for practical jokes. He spent far too much of his time in efforts to trap the press with no apparent goal other than to make reporters look foolish. The best remembered instance was his misdirection on the budget figures during his first year in office. He chortled with glee when several newsmen wrote that he had abandoned the struggle to keep the budget below $100,000,000,000 (b) and he was then able to drop a $98,000,000,000 (b) document in their laps. It was impossible for any member of the staff to make him understand that he was sacrificing credibility for the satisfaction of taunting a few journalists who had permitted him to "put one over" on them.

Much of this was traceable to his inability to connect press relations with the conduct of business. He thought of news as a hazard to commerce and government rather than a condition of social organization. In his judgment, the real affairs of the world were best conducted in secret where principals could get together and work out their differences. He did not think of public debate as a part of the governing process. It was rather a gauntlet which public officials had to run in order to serve the nation. Therefore, the objective of press relations was to divert press attention to other matters.

This led him to a ceaseless search for the public relations man who could shape the news as he wanted it to be shaped. Invariably, the man he had in mind was working for someone else. He was absolutely convinced that Pierre Salinger, for example, had elected John F. Kennedy President of the United States. Later he turned sour on Pierre—not for any Salinger deficiency but simply because he was expecting results that no living human being could deliver, and when they were not forthcoming, he decided he was being treated with bad faith.

There was a long succession of PR specialists, each convinced that his predecessor was a total incompetent. What they had not reckoned with was Lyndon Johnson. The irrationalities which they ascribed to lack of experience on the part of his staff came from LBJ himself.

Invariably, the "experts" retired in confusion while the regulars picked up the pieces.

Naturally, there were offsets. His skill in dealing with large numbers of people far outstripped his ineptitude in dealing with the press. In 1960, for example, he delivered a speech to the Liberal party convention in New York that assured him the permanent devotion of the workers in the garment trades. In 1964, he delivered a pro-civil rights speech in New Orleans which black leaders even today discuss in reverent tones. He could retain the allegiance of businessmen while pushing them to hire more minority employees, and he could secure the support of public utility officers while promoting the cause of public power.

Campaign Liability

In 1964, Barry Goldwater did not have a chance—not because his public relations were poor but because he was up against a master politician. In retrospect, it is fair to say that Lyndon Johnson's efforts at public relations invariably set his campaigning back. His staff found itself conducting a continuous salvage operation. The fervent desire of the White House press staff was that he stay in the White House and tend to business—or, at least, that he stay away from the press.

Unlike Mrs. Johnson, who had an uncanny knack for saying precisely the right thing at the right time, LBJ was incredibly clumsy when talking to a group of journalists. He could project overpowering charm in a face-to-face conversation with one reporter, but it deserted him when he faced a group of any size. At times he could become a droning bore and at other times he could convert a normal, even praiseworthy, thought into a shocking declaration which he did not intend to make. In the aftermath of the Walter Jenkins case, for example, he appeared to be counterattacking the Republican party for having had some homosexuals in its midst when he was only trying to say that homosexuality was not, and should not be, a partisan issue.

Another problem arose out of his lack of a sense of humor. He was a practical joker and a talented mimic. But he could not see the ludicrous, as it applied to him. In the Bobby Baker case, for instance, two facts were clear:

1. He had taken a deep personal interest in Bobby and had been responsible for his rapid promotion to secretary of the Senate Majority.

2. There was no credible evidence that he had ever participated consciously in the events that led to Bobby's conviction.

Unfortunately, LBJ decided that the way to handle the matter was to refute the general press description of Baker as a Johnson protégé. He seized upon a technicality—that Bobby had been elected to his post by *all* the Senate Democrats—and used it as a base for a claim that he hardly knew Bobby Baker. The election had been pro forma and had taken place during a period when Johnson could have persuaded the Senate to pass a resolution abolishing Congress. The press roared—with laughter, not anger—and reporters spent weeks telling each other "I hardly knew Bobby Baker" jokes. Underneath the amusement, however, was a strong suspicion that there must be something to "cover up" when a President was willing to resort to so flimsy a story.

Press Conferences

It may have been his inability to sell the press such things as the Bobby Baker story that led to the press conference problems. He was extraordinarily reluctant to hold them—which was rather surprising in view of the fact that he handled substantive questions well. He possessed an astonishing grasp of the operations of the government. His head was crammed with statistics on the economy and the society. He had his fingers on every negotiation in the field of foreign affairs. On such matters, it was virtually impossible to catch him napping. At least in the early days, before his political instincts deserted him, he knew his business and he could articulate it.

Nevertheless, it was virtually impossible to persuade him to hold an announced press conference. He preferred impromptu affairs—presumably because they did not afford reporters time to think up "mean" questions. In the early days of his presidency, some of these were quite successful because they were at least held in his office where there was an opportunity to take coherent notes. Later, however, he took to inviting the press on long walks around the White House grounds. These were sheer madness—a press corps 30 to 40 strong following him at a jog trot and elbowing each other for position where they could catch a few words.

There were undeniable virtues to the impromptu press conferences in his office. They had all the charm of spontaneity and afforded a genuine opportunity to explore his thinking (insofar as a man's thinking can be explored through questions). But the press—especially the electronic press—needed the announced, formal conference as well. On these, he really dug in his heels. It was rare for him to hold one unless it was tied to a gimmick. The famous "Children's Press Conference" at the White House, to which the sons and daughters of journalists were invited, was not really a publicity stunt. It was an inspiration of a desperate press secretary who found it the only path to a badly needed press conference.

The preparations for press conferences were simply unbelievable. They included a series of meetings with the press officers of the government who would submit lists of potential questions and possible answers. These would be narrowed down by the White House press staff and then considered at a Cabinet meeting. The culmination was in the East Room of the White House where LBJ would mount the rostrum with a press briefing book which he would promptly, and sensibly, forget. He would come up with his own answers and they were generally superior to those which had been supplied. I finally came to the conclusion that the traditional White House press conference preparatory system was nothing but a baby's security blanket. It played a useful role in soothing the nerves of the President, and that was all it did.

Lessons Unlearned

For some reason which I never fully fathomed, his real triumphs at formal press conferences did not encourage him to repeat the process. Instead, he spent considerable time at informal sessions trying to persuade journalists that they were wrong in asking him to hold them. His principal argument was that he could not schedule a conference in advance because there might not be any news for him to announce on the appointed day. He thought this argument was conclusive and could not understand why it was not bought. A number of journalists tried to explain to him that the purpose of a press conference was to ask questions rather than to receive announcements. He regarded this as pure sophistry.

On this issue, however, I suspect that there was something deeper than misunderstanding of the workings of the press. LBJ had an abhorrence of schedules. He regarded them as unconscionable intrusions upon his right to freedom of choice. Announcements of trips had to be forced from him, and what he really wanted to do was reveal a journey after he had arrived at his destination. This was quite a hardship upon the White House press corps whose members did not know whether to bring a packed bag with them when they came to work in the morning. They got little help from the Press Office, as I was in the same predicament. My only advantage was that I knew him better and could guess.

There were more serious problems than the convenience of the press. During 1964, he was scheduled to make the traditional

Democratic Labor Day speech in Detroit. He refused to either confirm or deny that he was going to do it. We arrived in Detroit that Monday morning to encounter the most deserted streets I have seen in my experience with American cities. Detroit's automobile workers had been given no reason to remain in town. Therefore, they had packed picnic baskets and headed for the countryside. After that, we were at least able to get political campaign schedules announced.

To a certain extent, this tied in to his refusal to regard the press as an organization having structure and machinery. He thought that a newspaper was something that appeared on the front doorstep every morning and a television newscast was something that happened when a switch was flicked. He was never clear on the process by which stories were written, edited, set up in type, printed, and eventually delivered to the consumer. This confusion left him with the belief that press relations were entirely a matter of "selling" newsmen and women on a point of view. The equally important process of making it possible for the journalist to operate was something that he scorned as "bagcarrying."

At one point, he even maneuvered himself into a position of filibustering his own stories. This occurred during the period of the unscheduled Saturday morning press conferences. I believe they happened originally because he felt lonely in the White House and, having nothing else to do, called a press conference. The first one was a great success because it was a novelty. Therefore, he repeated it the following Saturday and after a few weeks it became almost standard. Eventually, I convinced him that for a variety of reasons he did not get sufficient coverage out of them and they were dropped.

The biggest problem with them, however, was that he simply would not let the press go. He would start out with two or three fairly major announcements—the kind that made reporters itch to get to their typewriters. On Saturday, the time element is extremely important as deadlines are early. This was explained to him on several occasions, but it made no difference. He would continue to talk almost up to the deadline when the staff would break it up. On each of these occasions, he would look upon us as bullies taking candy away from a baby. He was convinced that in a few more minutes, he would have made the biggest "sale" to the press in history.

The trouble was that there were always a "few more minutes." They never achieved "the big sale" for him, but they did lose a large share of the goodwill that he had built up in the first 20 minutes. He was entirely capable of charming a group of men into absolute adoration in half an hour and equally capable of parting with them as implacable enemies at the end of an hour. He did not know how to let well enough alone.

If all of this sounds confused, the answer is that it was confused. Orderly press relations and Lyndon Johnson were mutually exclusive concepts. To me, he is the final and irrefutable answer to those who believe that good press relations are essential to political success. If that were true, he could not have been elected sheriff of Blanco County.

I hasten to add that I do not despise good press relations. The communications expert is becoming more and more of a necessity in a society where communications are necessarily conducted through the mass media. But I believe that the expert must have something to communicate and that it takes more than press technique to win a campaign. Otherwise, how could Lyndon Johnson have ever won a presidential campaign—even against Barry Goldwater?

CONCLUDING OBSERVATIONS

It may be that the relations between the President and the press, to paraphrase Clemenceau, are too important to be left to politicians and journalists. If so, colloquia and discussions such as the ones at the Miller Center resulting in the present volume should be multiplied in universities around the country. The weight of the discussion in the papers and exchanges presented here make clear at least some of the dimensions of the problem. They provide a valuable introduction to the issues.

We have tried in two successive Markle volumes to bring to the surface some of the views of leading White House press corps and former press secretaries. To reconcile some of the ideas put forward by each "estate" would require a far wider discussion. Yet the beginnings of such a discussion are set forth in broad outline in the two volumes. The assumptions and responsibilities of the two groups as they see them plainly determine their viewpoints on a number of critical issues. Not only do their attitudes invite further elaboration if not debate but the whole problem deserves long-term study by serious researchers and scholars. Thus the value of the two books is both immediate in promoting wider public understanding and long-term in providing data and information for future research studies.